Prioritizing
the
Common
Core

D1405581

Prioritizing
the
Common
Core

*Identifying Specific Standards
to Emphasize the Most*

► LARRY AINSWORTH ◄

LEAD+
LEARN
PRESS

ENGLEWOOD, COLORADO

The Leadership and Learning Center
317 Inverness Way South, Suite 150
Englewood, Colorado 80112
Phone 1.866.399.6019 | Fax 303.504.9417
www.leadandlearn.com

Copyright © 2013 The Leadership and Learning Center
All rights reserved.

Published by Lead + Learn Press, a division of Houghton Mifflin Harcourt.

Note: Every attempt was made to obtain permission for reprint/use of contributors' work. No part of this publication may be reproduced, stored in a retrieval system, or transmitted in any form or by any means, electronic, mechanical, photocopying, recording, scanning, or otherwise, except as permitted by law, without the prior written permission of the publisher.

Limited Reproduction Permission: Permission is hereby granted to the purchaser of this book to reproduce the forms for educational and noncommercial use only.

Notice of Liability: The information in this book is distributed on an "as is" basis, without warranty. While every precaution has been taken in the preparation of the book, neither the authors nor Houghton Mifflin Harcourt shall have any liability to any person or entity with respect to any loss or damage caused or alleged to be caused directly or indirectly by the instructions contained in this book.

All Web links in this book are correct as of the publication date but may have become inactive or otherwise modified since that time. If you notice a deactivated or changed link, please notify the publisher and specify the Web link, the book title, and the page number on which the link appears so that corrections may be made in future editions.

Lead + Learn Press also publishes books in a variety of electronic formats. Some content that appears in print may not be available in electronic books.

Library of Congress Cataloging-in-Publication Data

    Ainsworth, Larry.
      Prioritizing the common core : identifying specific standards to emphasize the most / Larry Ainsworth.
        pages   cm
      Includes bibliographical references and index.
      ISBN 978-1-935588-41-2 (alk. paper)
    1. Education—Standards—United States.   I. Title.
      LB3060.83.A385 2013
      379.1'580973—dc23

                                                    2013018492

ISBN 978-1-935588-41-2

Printed in the United States of America

17 16 15 14 13   02 03 04 05 06 07

I respectfully dedicate this book to the educators and leaders in every school district, educational service agency, and state department of education within the 46 states and the District of Columbia that are transitioning from state standards to the Common Core. My hope is that the practical and proven process presented in these pages will do much to help you effectively focus your standards, curriculum, instruction, and assessment practices to better prepare your students for success—not only on the rigorous new national assessments, but ultimately in college, career, and in life itself.

Prioritizing the Common Core

the

Common

Core

Identifying Specific Standards
to Emphasize the Most

► LARRY AINSWORTH ◄

LEAD+
LEARN
PRESS

ENGLEWOOD, COLORADO

The Leadership and Learning Center
317 Inverness Way South, Suite 150
Englewood, Colorado 80112
Phone 1.866.399.6019 | Fax 303.504.9417
www.leadandlearn.com

Copyright © 2013 The Leadership and Learning Center
All rights reserved.

Published by Lead + Learn Press, a division of Houghton Mifflin Harcourt.

Note: Every attempt was made to obtain permission for reprint/use of contributors' work. No part of this publication may be reproduced, stored in a retrieval system, or transmitted in any form or by any means, electronic, mechanical, photocopying, recording, scanning, or otherwise, except as permitted by law, without the prior written permission of the publisher.

Limited Reproduction Permission: Permission is hereby granted to the purchaser of this book to reproduce the forms for educational and noncommercial use only.

Notice of Liability: The information in this book is distributed on an "as is" basis, without warranty. While every precaution has been taken in the preparation of the book, neither the authors nor Houghton Mifflin Harcourt shall have any liability to any person or entity with respect to any loss or damage caused or alleged to be caused directly or indirectly by the instructions contained in this book.

All Web links in this book are correct as of the publication date but may have become inactive or otherwise modified since that time. If you notice a deactivated or changed link, please notify the publisher and specify the Web link, the book title, and the page number on which the link appears so that corrections may be made in future editions.

Lead + Learn Press also publishes books in a variety of electronic formats. Some content that appears in print may not be available in electronic books.

Library of Congress Cataloging-in-Publication Data

Ainsworth, Larry.
    Prioritizing the common core : identifying specific standards to emphasize the
most / Larry Ainsworth.
        pages   cm
    Includes bibliographical references and index.
    ISBN 978-1-935588-41-2 (alk. paper)
    1. Education—Standards—United States.   I. Title.
    LB3060.83.A385 2013
    379.1'580973—dc23
                                                                                2013018492

ISBN 978-1-935588-41-2

Printed in the United States of America

17 16 15 14 13   02 03 04 05 06 07

I respectfully dedicate this book to the educators and leaders in every school district, educational service agency, and state department of education within the 46 states and the District of Columbia that are transitioning from state standards to the Common Core. My hope is that the practical and proven process presented in these pages will do much to help you effectively focus your standards, curriculum, instruction, and assessment practices to better prepare your students for success—not only on the rigorous new national assessments, but ultimately in college, career, and in life itself.

CONTENTS

LIST OF FIGURES

ABOUT THE AUTHOR

 **Larry Ainsworth** is the Executive Director of Professional Development at The Leadership and Learning Center in Englewood, Colorado, U.S.A. He travels nationally and internationally to assist school systems in implementing best practices related to standards, assessment, curriculum, and instruction across all grades and content areas. He is the author or coauthor of 12 published books, including: *Rigorous Curriculum Design* (2010), *"Unwrapping" the Standards* (2003b), *Power Standards* (2003a), *Common Formative Assessments* (2006), *Five Easy Steps to a Balanced Math Program* (2000 and 2006), *Student Generated Rubrics* (1998), and, his most recent coauthored title, *Getting Started with Rigorous Curriculum Design: How School Districts Are Successfully Redesigning Their Curricula for the Common Core* (2013). Since 1999, Larry has worked on-site in school systems to assist leaders and educators in understanding and implementing standards-based practices: prioritizing and "unwrapping" state standards and Common Core standards, developing common formative assessments, designing authentic performance tasks, and creating rigorous curricular units of study in all content areas, pre-kindergarten through grade 12.

Larry has delivered keynote addresses and breakout sessions across North America and in Latin America. In 2012, the San Diego Unified School District, nineteenth largest public school system in the United States, selected Larry's curriculum model, *Rigorous Curriculum Design*, to recreate district K–12 English language arts and mathematics curricula to align with the Common Core. Larry is leading their educators in the development of rigorous units of study that will be implemented in San Diego schools during the 2013/14 school year.

With 24 years of experience as an upper elementary and middle school classroom teacher in demographically diverse schools, Larry brings a varied background and wide range of professional experiences to each of his presentations. He has held numerous leadership roles within school districts, including mentor teacher and K–12 math committee cochair, and has served as a mathematics assessment consultant in several San Diego County school districts. Larry holds a Master of Science degree in educational administration.

ACKNOWLEDGMENTS

I am indebted to the following state, district, and regional education service agencies for the opportunity they provided me to personally lead their educators and leaders through the process of prioritizing the Common Core: Connecticut Department of Education; Washington, D.C., Office of the State Superintendent of Education; San Diego Unified School District, San Diego, California; Northwest Regional ESD, Hillsboro, Oregon; Community Consolidated School District 64, Park Ridge, Illinois; Tully Central School District, Tully, New York; West Hartford Public Schools, West Hartford, Connecticut; Central Unified School District, Fresno, California; and Colorado Springs District 11, Colorado.

I would also like to especially acknowledge and thank those educators and leaders who gave of their time, thought, and energy to contribute to this publication:

Amy Gregory Young, Ph.D., District Testing Coordinator, Greenwood School District 50, Greenwood, South Carolina

Jackie Blosser, Title I Coordinator/Curriculum Team Leader Reading-Language Arts/District Test Coordinator, and Cathy Collins, Math Curriculum Team Leader, Lima City Schools, Lima, Ohio

Lissa Pijanowski, Ed.D., Former Associate Superintendent, Forsyth County Schools, Cumming, Georgia

Sally Alubicki, Ed.D., Director of Teaching and Assessment, and Paul Vicinus, Director of Secondary Education, West Hartford Public Schools, West Hartford, Connecticut

Karen Brofft, Ed.S., Assistant Superintendent, Englewood Schools, Englewood, Colorado

Art Anderson, Director of School Improvement and Instruction, Northwest Regional Education Service District, Hillsboro, Oregon; Marta Turner, Pam Hallvik, Karen Durbin, and Ann Kelsey, NWRESD School Improvement Specialists; and Sharron Selman, Math Consultant.

Special thanks to my professional development associate colleagues at The Leadership and Learning Center: Jan Christinson, Lori Cook, and Lisa Cebelak, who reviewed this manuscript and offered helpful clarifications; Stephen Ventura, Laura Benson, and Kara Vandas who led four of the six school districts profiled in this book through the prioritization process.

INTRODUCTION

"Now I must teach and assess my students' understanding of the Common Core State Standards, and they are even *more rigorous* than our state standards were!" This is the new challenge facing our educators and school leaders in the 46 states and the District of Columbia that have adopted the Common Core State Standards (CCSS).

These educators need practical and proven strategies, not only to help students learn the English language arts and mathematics Common Core, but also to reaffirm in them a renewed sense of confidence and optimism: "We CAN do this!"

If you or your colleagues are

- feeling overwhelmed by the instructional implications of the Common Core,

- realizing you have too little classroom time to effectively teach and assess these more rigorous standards,

- wondering how you can meet the diverse range of student learning needs in relation to the CCSS,

then this book will offer you a practical and proven method to help manage these challenges.

A Formidable Set of Challenges

School systems throughout the nation today face a formidable set of challenges. Four of these challenges in particular relate directly to standards, high-stakes tests, and instruction.

First, many students have not been learning at levels high enough to demonstrate proficiency on standards-based *state* assessments.

Second, the *state* standards at each grade level contain more concepts and skills than students can realistically learn within the course of one school year. Educators who lack proven strategies for managing the volume of standards have had to "pick and choose" the ones they believe will most benefit their students. This has led to inconsistencies as to which standards are emphasized and which are not. Such an approach can negatively impact student performance on high-stakes assessments if the "wrong" standards are targeted. To safeguard this from happening, educators feel that they must "cover" *all* the standards with less than optimum depth.

Third, those who teach in school districts that have "powered," or prioritized, their state standards often admit to focusing *only* on those state-tested standards, partially or completing ignoring the other ones.

Fourth, educators believe their academic freedom to make professional decisions about what their students need to learn is being eclipsed in what they perceive to be a move toward *standardization of their instruction*, rather than an effective implementation of *standards* to improve both instruction and student achievement on all assessment measures.

The Challenges of the Common Core

The Common Core State Standards for English language arts and mathematics are now the singular focus of American education in all but four states. The CCSS specify *what* K–12 students are expected to know and be able to do at each grade level by the end of the school year. Because these standards have been vertically "spiraled" from one grade to the next, with learning progressions carefully built into their design, the expectation is that all students will (must) learn them by the end of each school year to be prepared for the standards at the *next* grade level or course. This means that the prior grade's standards will become *prerequisites* for students to be successful at the next level of learning.

When the new national assessments to measure student attainment of the CCSS—now being developed by the Smarter Balanced Assessment Consortium (SBAC) and the Partnership for Assessment of Readiness for College and Careers (PARCC)—are first administered in 2014/15, we will find out how successful we have been in preparing students for these new end-of-year tests in grades 3 through 11, and where we still need to improve in order to move *all* students toward higher proficiency in the years that follow. Since the new assessments will be directly aligned to the Common Core, these standards have naturally become the critical focus for achieving the results that our educators will be expected to produce.

Even though the federal reauthorization of the Elementary and Secondary Education Act of 2001—"No Child Left Behind"—remains in limbo, and states are seeking and being granted waivers for reporting AYP ("adequate yearly progress") results, the tracking of student achievement data on annual standardized tests is now a regular part of our educational culture. School systems will continue to set and strive to meet student proficiency goals for *all* student sub-groups. The expectations of the CCSS are quite specific in requiring that *all* students, including those with learning disabilities and those with limited English proficiency, receive equal access to the new standards. In addition, since teacher evaluations in many states are now tied to student performance on standardized tests, the accountability pressures confronting educators and leaders can only increase.

The CCSS, internationally benchmarked to educational standards in high-performing nations around the world, are much more cognitively demanding than the state standards that most American educators are used to. The old "coverage" model of instruction will no longer work. Our educators must be able to sharply focus instruction, assessment, and curriculum on those identified standards that represent the "end game"—the ones that are the *most rigorous* or *comprehensive for that grade level or course*—not those that are merely foundational or baseline. These carefully selected CCSS are the standards that must be emphasized the most.

What *Are* Priority Standards?

"Power Standards," a term coined in the 1990s by Dr. Douglas Reeves, founder of The Leadership and Learning Center, refers to those grade- or course-specific standards that are critical for student success. By his own definition, Power Standards are "those standards that, once mastered, give a student the ability to use reasoning and thinking skills to learn and understand other curriculum objectives" (Ainsworth, 2003a, p. 7). The term "Power Standards" is often used synonymously with the more self-explanatory terms "Priority Standards" and "Essential Standards."

Priority Standards are a carefully selected *subset* of the total list of the grade-specific and course-specific standards within each content area that students must know and be able to do by the end of each school year in order to be prepared for the standards in the next grade level or course. Priority Standards represent the *assured student competencies* that each teacher needs to help every student learn, and demonstrate proficiency in, prior to leaving the current grade or course.

All other standards are referred to as *supporting* standards—those standards that support, connect to, or enhance the Priority Standards. They are taught within the context of the Priority Standards, but do not receive the same degree of instruction and assessment emphasis as do the Priority Standards. The supporting standards often become the *instructional scaffolds* to help students understand and attain the more rigorous and comprehensive Priority Standards. Every standard, whether it is a state standard or a Common Core State Standard, is ultimately classified as either "priority" or "supporting." The one exception is the "Overarching Goal Statement," described in Chapter Two.

When the Priority Standards are carefully selected through school and/or district consensus, educators teach these particular standards for depth of student understanding using curriculum developed toward that end. Students demonstrate what they have learned on meaningful assessments—classroom, common, and district benchmarks—intentionally aligned to the Priority Standards. Educators systematically collect, examine, and use this formative student data to diagnose student learning needs and then to differentiate their instruction for individual students *prior to* summative assessments. Collectively, these assessments *for* learning (formative, in-process), when closely aligned to assessments *of* learning (summative end-of-course, end-of-year), provide the evidence of the degree of student attainment of the Priority Standards.

This intentional alignment between formative and summative assessments needs to extend to the SBAC and PARCC assessments as well. Educators should align their in-school formative assessments to the formats and rigor of the summative SBAC and PARCC prototype test questions so that students will be able to "make the transfer" of what they know and can do to these new and as yet unfamiliar national assessments.

The Problem Was the Quantity

During the past decade, the need to prioritize the state standards was driven primarily by the unrealistic numbers of grade-specific standards that educators were supposed to teach, assess, reteach, and reassess within a finite number of days (typically 170–180) each academic school year.

Three random examples of state standards illustrate this point. Figures I.1, I.2, and I.3 show the numbers of grade-specific or course-specific *state* standards in the identified content areas and grades along with the grade-by-grade totals. Not only do these sizeable numbers represent instruction and assessment challenges for the educators, but imagine the challenges these numbers mean to students who must learn *all* of these standards in every content area *each year*. For students needing any kind of ongoing specialized instruction (remediation, intervention, special education, or English language support), the challenge for them becomes even greater.

FIGURE I.1	**Number of State Standards by Grade Level and Course (Example 1)**			
Grade	**English Language Arts**	**Math**	**Science**	**Totals**
Pre-K	56	22	18	**96**
K	73	35	20	**128**
1	90	39	23	**152**
2	93	42	21	**156**
3	91	43	23	**157**
4	91	44	25	**160**
5	79	49	31	**159**
6	66	45	36	**147**
7	61	46	26	**133**
8	62	46	29	**137**

FIGURE I.2	Number of State Standards by Grade Level and Course (Example 2)							

Grade	English Language Arts	Grade/ Course	Math	Grade/ Course	Science	Grade/ Course	Social Studies	Totals
K	71	K	35	K	31	K	38	175
1	99	1	39	1	30	1	51	219
2	95	2	40	2	29	2	51	215
3	100	3	43	3	32	3	59	234
4	80	4	42	4	31	4	79	232
5	94	5	38	5	39	5	87	258
6	87	6	39	6	41	6	73	240
7	90	7	43	7	40	7	79	252
8	63	8	43	8	43	8	108	257
9	81	Algebra I	42	Integrated	42	World Geography	66	231
10	84	Geometry	37	Biology	48	World History	81	250
11	81	Algebra II	44	Chemistry	49	U.S. History	92	266
12	84	Pre-Calculus	23	Physics	35	Government	81	223

| FIGURE I.3 | Number of State Standards by Grade Level and Course (Example 3) |

Grade	Math	English Language Arts	Science	Social Studies	Sub-Total	Arts	Physical Education	Health	Grand Totals
K	21	60	9		90				**90**
1	32	76	13		121				**121**
2	61	78	11		150				**150**
3	57	96	16	18	187	12	7	16	**222**
4	62	106	15		183				**183**
5	58	110	16	80	264	12	8	18	**302**
6	70	107	15		192				**192**
7	64	105	16		185				**185**
8	66	104	17	108	295	12	13	24	**344**
9–12	85	142	35	116	378	12	14	40	**444**

A Research-Supported Rationale

Prioritizing the standards makes sense from a logical and practitioner's perspective, but the concept is also widely supported by the published writings of educational researchers and thought leaders. Here is a representative sample of compelling statements in support of prioritizing the standards:

- Douglas Reeves: "Because of the limitations of time and the extraordinary variety in learning backgrounds of students, teachers and leaders need focus and clarity in order to prepare their students for success. Power [Priority] Standards help to provide that focus and clarity" (Reeves, 2001, p. 167).

- W. James Popham: "Teachers need to prioritize a set of content standards so they can identify the content standards for which they will devote powerful thoroughgoing instruction, and then they need to formally and systematically assess student mastery of only those high-priority content standards" (Popham, 2003, p. 36).

- W. James Popham: "Reduce the number of eligible-to-be-assessed curricular aims so that (1) teachers are not overwhelmed by too many instructional targets, and (2) a student's mastery of each curricular aim that's assessed can be determined with reasonable accuracy. Teachers who can focus their instructional attention on a modest number of truly significant skills usually can get their students to master those skills—even if the skills are genuinely challenging" (Popham, 2004, p. 31).

- Heidi Hayes Jacobs: "Given the limited time you have with your students, curriculum design has become more and more an issue of deciding what you won't teach as well as what you will teach. You cannot do it all. As a designer, you must choose the essential" (Jacobs, 1997).

As Donald Viegut and I reported in our book *Common Formative Assessments* (Corwin Press, 2006), educational researcher Robert Marzano (Sherer, 2001) determined the amount of instructional time educators would need to effectively teach all the state standards students are expected to learn by the end of high school:

- 5.6 instructional hours per day x 180 days in a typical academic year = 1,008 hours per year x 13 years = **13,104** total hours of K–12 instruction.

- McREL (Mid-continent Research for Education and Learning) identified 200 standards and 3,093 benchmarks (grade-specific learning outcomes) in national- and state-level documents across 14 different subject areas.

- Classroom teachers estimated a need for **15,465** hours to adequately teach them all. (Sherer, 2001)

Marzano went on to calculate how many of those hours each school day are actually dedicated to instruction of students:

- Varies widely from a low of 21 percent to a high of 69 percent.

- Taking the highest estimate of 69 percent, only 9,042 hours are actually available for instruction out of the original 13,104 total hours.

- Can 200 standards and 3,093 benchmarks needing 15,465 hours be taught in only 9,042 hours of instructional time? No! (Sherer, 2001)

Marzano concluded these statistics with a memorable assertion based on his research: "To cover all this content, you would have to change schooling from K–12 to K–22." He recommended a fractional guideline for reducing the number of standards: "By my reckoning, we would have to cut content by about two-thirds." He then declared, "The sheer number of standards is the biggest impediment to implementing standards" (Scherer, 2001, p. 15).

Even though Dr. Marzano's research was based on *state* standards, and not the Common Core, it pointed out the critical need to prioritize voluminous numbers of standards as a way to sharply focus instruction, assessment, and curriculum. Why there is a real need to prioritize the *Common Core* will be the focus of Chapter One.

About *Prioritizing the Common Core*

Power Standards: Identifying the Standards that Matter the Most (Ainsworth, 2003a) was based on my own experience leading educators and leaders through the prioritization process of *state* standards. Since that time, thousands of educators and leaders have continued to prioritize state standards in multiple content areas and grade levels using the systematic process explained in that first volume.

Prioritizing the Common Core: Identifying Specific Standards to Emphasize the Most updates that proven, step-by-step process as it applies to the rigor of the

English language arts and mathematics Common Core State Standards. After a decade of experience in leading groups of educators and leaders across the United States through this proven way of prioritizing state standards—and throughout the past two years in prioritizing the Common Core—I hope this new book will provide schools, school districts, regions, and states clear and effective guidelines to successfully replicate this same powerful practice with the CCSS.

Chapter One presents an in-depth explanation of the rationale for prioritizing the Common Core, including the total numbers of grade- and course-specific CCSS in English language arts and literacy and in mathematics. Chapter Two explains the step-by-step process to prioritize the K–12 English language arts and literacy Common Core. Chapter Three explains how to apply that same process to the K–8 and high school mathematics Common Core. Because there is a need to involve as many stakeholders as possible in this important decision-making process, Chapter Four offers practical strategies for soliciting feedback and input from those not involved in the initial selections of the Priority Standards prior to the final determination of those selections.

Chapters Five through Ten provide narrative summaries of the processes six different school districts in six different states have used to identify their Priority CCSS, written by those who directed the work. These chapter authors have provided their contact information should readers wish to contact them for further information. A few have posted their districts' Priority Common Core Standards on their Web sites.

Due to space limitations in this book, full examples of Priority Common Core Standards identified by these six school systems could not be included. This is actually a benefit. Leaders in every school system you will read about have echoed that the *process* of prioritizing the CCSS and the K–12 vertical discussions that took place between and among their own educators may well have been of greater value than the actual finished products themselves. Because of this, I strongly recommend that the selection of Priority CCSS be a decision made, however possible, by the educators in each school system, region, or state—even though it requires an investment of time and personnel to do so. This will make it easier for those same educators to revisit and update their selections as new information emerges about how these standards will be assessed by PARCC and SBAC. It will save them time in "getting to know" the new standards relevant to their own instructional programs because they will have already studied them during prioritization.

Chapter Eleven presents the Priority Standards process in a concise, step-by-step checklist format. This checklist can serve as an easy reference for groups of educators and leaders as they work through their own identification of the Priority Standards.

Chapter Twelve explains how prioritizing the Common Core is the first of five foundational steps for designing rigorous curricular units of study to meet the instructional shifts and assessment demands of the CCSS and prepare students for success on the new national assessments.

A Reader's Assignment at the conclusion of Chapters One through Four will help you immediately apply the information specific to that chapter. Utilizing these Reader's Assignments, you and your colleagues can successfully identify your own Priority Common Core Standards when you are ready to do so.

Prioritizing the Common Core will greatly benefit school and district leaders, classroom educators, curriculum coordinators, and instructional resource specialists in determining which CCSS are the most important to emphasize—a critical first step in preparing students for success in college and career, in life, and on all high-stakes assessments they will encounter in the coming years.

CHAPTER ONE

Why Prioritize the Common Core State Standards?

The Rationale for Priority Standards

The consensus among educators nationwide is that in-depth instruction paired with focused assessment of *essential* concepts and skills is far more effective than superficially "covering" every concept and skill listed in the standards. Owing to the limitations of time and the wide diversity in learning backgrounds of today's students, educators are faced with the almost insurmountable task of trying to teach all the standards for their particular grade and content areas while at the same time meeting the extraordinary range of student learning needs.

Educators agree *in principle* that a sharper focus on fewer standards would dramatically improve student learning, but they feel unable to do this in practice because there are so many standards to cover for the annual high-stakes test. The reality is that intensive preparation for standardized tests continues to drive instruction in classrooms across America.

When teaching becomes reduced to this kind of high-pressure, frantic coverage approach to test preparation, serious questions arise:

1. What effect does this have on teacher and student motivation?

2. What does this do to the quality of teaching and associated student learning activities?

3. What impact does this have on student readiness/preparedness for the next level of learning?

Whenever I have asked educators if all of their students came to them prepared to learn their particular grade's state standards, the answer has invariably been "No." When I ask them why they think that is the case, they reply with a host of responses that include but are not limited to the following: lack of motivation on the part of the students, high student mobility, challenges related to second language acquisition, complex student learning needs, and ineffective instruction in prior grades.

Certainly there are numerous factors that contribute to our students not being completely prepared for each new grade. Certain of these factors are beyond our individual or collective control. However, we need to identify those probable causes we *can* control and address them in a systematic way.

One Cause We Can Control

If instruction each year is reduced to racing students through an "inch-deep, mile-wide" exposure to standards, surely this must be one of the main reasons why students often do not remember what they learned last year. The resulting lack of readiness for the current year's standards thus necessitates a time-consuming review and reteaching of concepts and skills that students "should have learned" in prior grades. The cumulative effect of this cycle being repeated over several years begs the question, "Unless we change the way we teach the standards, how can we ever expect to see different results?"

By emphasizing depth over breadth, we can do much to help students retain what they have been taught. Educators can then provide learning experiences around a *prioritized* set of standards that requires students to utilize higher-order thinking skills and integrate present learning with prior knowledge.

The Rigorous Demands of the Common Core

The Common Core State Standards are based upon a mastery model of learning: students must demonstrate proficiency in the standards by the *end of each grade level* in order to be prepared for the standards at the next grade level. "Each standard was selected only when the best available evidence indicated that its mastery was essential for college and career readiness in a 21st-century globally competitive society" (http://www.corestandards.org/).

The promise of the Common Core is that *all* students should be held to the *same* high expectations. For students learning English as a second language, educators must "provide additional time, appropriate instructional support, and aligned assessments as they acquire both English language proficiency and content area knowledge." This same high expectation extends to our students with special needs:

"Supports and accommodations should ensure that students receive access to multiple means of learning and opportunities to demonstrate knowledge, but retain the rigor and high expectations of the Common Core State Standards" (http://www.corestandards.org/).

The Need to Prioritize the Common Core

In Chapter Five of *Rigorous Curriculum Design* (Ainsworth, 2010), I presented what I believe to be a persuasive case for prioritizing the Common Core State Standards. I based my assertions on the *numbers* and *rigor* of the English language arts grade-specific standards, and on the *fewer but decidedly more rigorous* mathematics grade- and course-specific standards. My experience over the past two years in leading district, regional, and statewide groups of educators and leaders through this highly collaborative process has confirmed the need to prioritize—not the broad anchor standards that span all grades, but rather the standards *specific to each grade*. Included here are several key points from *Rigorous Curriculum Design* that support the rationale for doing so.

Fewer, Clearer, Higher

In 2008, Sir Michael Barber, onetime chief advisor to former British Prime Minister Tony Blair, stated: "The question of national standards is inescapable. The U.S. needs *fewer, clearer, and higher* national standards" (Klein, 2008, p. 24). This made good sense. *Clearer* is synonymous with "specific and understandable," and *higher* signifies "rigorous and more challenging." But it was the other adjective—"fewer"— that particularly caught my attention. If *fewer* meant "less than what we currently find in state standards," then these Common Core State Standards should make it much more doable for U.S. educators to meet the difficult challenge of adequately teaching, assessing, reteaching, and reassessing their students on *all* of the CCSS within each academic school year. This would certainly be welcome news to educators who have for years tried valiantly (and in vain) to ensure their students learn and demonstrate proficiency on *all* of the state standards.

When I first began reading the published versions of the English language arts and mathematics CCSS, one question was uppermost in my mind: If there are indeed fewer standards, will prioritization still be necessary? Having witnessed for many years the challenge of educators all over the country needing to prioritize voluminous numbers of state standards, I was naturally hopeful that the answer would be "no"—for the sake of educators *and* their students. Then I read that any state that adopted the CCSS could also add an *extra fifteen percent* from their existing state standards. This meant *more* standards, not fewer! Still, I remained optimistic.

Organization of the Common Core ELA and Literacy Standards

In English language arts, there are 32 College and Career Readiness (CCR) anchor standards divided into four main literacy strands—*reading* (including literature, informational text, and K–5 foundational skills), *writing, speaking and listening,* and *language.* The reading strand has ten CCR anchor standards, the writing strand has ten, the speaking and listening strand has six, and the language strand has six. Each set of anchor standards defines the broad K–12 literacy expectations for college and career readiness (summarized by Maryann D. Wiggs, 2011, p. 27).

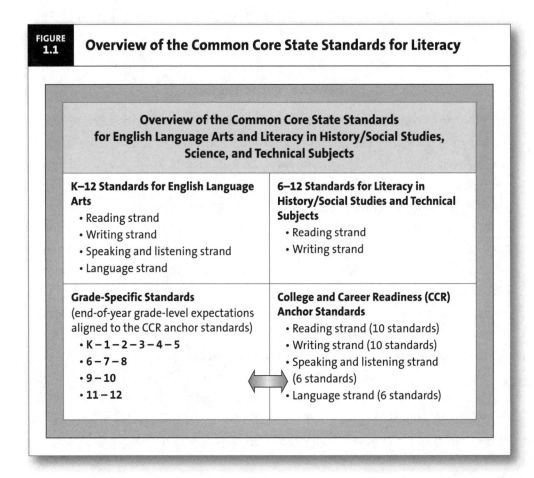

FIGURE 1.1 Overview of the Common Core State Standards for Literacy

Overview of the Common Core State Standards for English Language Arts and Literacy in History/Social Studies, Science, and Technical Subjects

K–12 Standards for English Language Arts
- Reading strand
- Writing strand
- Speaking and listening strand
- Language strand

6–12 Standards for Literacy in History/Social Studies and Technical Subjects
- Reading strand
- Writing strand

Grade-Specific Standards
(end-of-year grade-level expectations aligned to the CCR anchor standards)
- K – 1 – 2 – 3 – 4 – 5
- 6 – 7 – 8
- 9 – 10
- 11 – 12

College and Career Readiness (CCR) Anchor Standards
- Reading strand (10 standards)
- Writing strand (10 standards)
- Speaking and listening strand (6 standards)
- Language strand (6 standards)

Each *broad* anchor standard is accompanied by *grade-specific* standards for every individual grade, kindergarten through grade 8 and for the two high school grade bands, 9–10 and 11–12. These grade-level standards provide the specificity of what the corresponding anchor standards mean at each grade level. Together the anchor standards and their related, grade-specific standards explicitly define the knowledge and skills that students must know and be able to demonstrate proficiency in by the end of each grade in order to be prepared for the standards at the next grade level. Figure 1.1 shows an overview of the CCSS for English language arts and literacy.

What I found immediately impressive about the Common Core State Standards in English language arts is their overall clarity and specificity (*clearer*), their inherent rigor (*higher*), and particularly the *spiraled learning progressions* from grade to grade. Still to be determined, however, was the criterion most relevant to the issue of prioritization—*fewer*. The only way to determine this was to actually count them.

Counting the *Grade-Specific* ELA Standards

Figure 1.2 shows the numerical breakdown of the *grade-specific* ELA standards of the Common Core by grade levels and grade bands. I have listed the number of standards within each strand in separate columns and then added the columns together to show the total number of standards for each of these grades. I believe the totals speak for themselves in terms of whether or not prioritization is still needed—and these numbers do not take into account the *additional fifteen percent of state standards* that states are free to include.

Each of the literacy strands corresponds to several College and Career Readiness anchor standards—broadly worded statements supported by more specifically worded grade-level standards. Together these complementary statements "define the skills and understandings that all students must demonstrate." (www.corestandards .org/ELA-Literacy/CCRA/R). For example, here are the first two of ten CCR anchor standards for Reading in grades K–12:

> "Read closely to determine what the text says explicitly and to make logical inferences from it; cite specific textual evidence when writing or speaking to support conclusions drawn from the text."

> "Determine central ideas or themes of a text and analyze their development; summarize the key supporting details and ideas."

FIGURE 1.2	Common Core State Standards—English Language Arts						
Grade Level(s)	Literature	Informational Text	Foundational Skills	Writing	Speaking & Listening	Language	Total
Kinder-garten	10	10	17	7	8	21	**73**
Grade 1	10	10	19	7	9	27	**82**
Grade 2	10	10	11	7	9	25	**72**
Grade 3	10	10	9	21	10	31	**91**
Grade 4	9	10	6	25	10	26	**86**
Grade 5	9	10	6	25	10	24	**84**
Grade 6	9	10	—	28	10	22	**79**
Grade 7	9	10	—	28	10	19	**76**
Grade 8	9	10	—	28	10	21	**78**
Grades 9–10	9	10	—	28	10	18	**75**
Grades 11–12	9	10	—	28	10	17	**74**

The grade-level standards specify exactly what students must know and be able to do at each grade in order to achieve the broader CCRs.

The case could be argued that the more *generally worded* anchor standards do not need to be counted into the total number if the *more specifically worded* grade-level or grade-band standards present the same end learning outcomes in greater detail.

The case might also be argued that *similar* standards in the same strand are really just instructional scaffolds to achieve one or more of the more rigorous, comprehensive standards listed in that strand. If either of these two positions were taken, then it might indeed lessen the total number of standards presented here.

However, I respectfully argue that these number totals are justified. *All* of the standards—whether they be anchor or grade-specific, foundational or scaffolds to more rigorous ones—must *collectively* be the focus of instruction, curriculum, and assessment throughout each academic school year, K–12. Together they represent the full list of explicit learning outcomes students are to achieve by the end of each grade.

I present these numbers of standards for no other reason than to support my assertion that educators must be able to determine—through a thoughtful, collaborative process—those standards they consider *essential* for their students to know and be able to do by the end of each school year and course of study. Until there truly are *fewer* standards, the need to prioritize will remain. As Lisa Cebelak, my colleague at The Leadership and Learning Center who specializes in the ELA Common Core, points out: "The *rigor* of the CCSS is one of the key reasons these standards need to be prioritized. They are complex and will truly take a full year of teaching in order for most students to become proficient with them. Now that there is a much greater emphasis on literacy skills (and therefore higher critical thinking) than there was in the past, the need to prioritize and scaffold those prioritized standards throughout the year is absolutely necessary. Gone are the days of 'checking off a standard' addressed in the first unit of study and not revisiting it the entire rest of the year."

Literacy Standards for Science and Technical Subjects, History and Social Studies

The authors of the Common Core "insist" that literacy be a *shared responsibility* across all content areas. To this end, the K–5 literacy standards for history/social studies, science, and technical subjects are embedded within the K–5 content strands. However, reading and writing standards for grades 6–12 history/social studies, science, and technical subjects are presented separately (see Figure 1.3). These literacy standards are not intended to replace existing content standards in those content areas, but rather to *supplement* them. Secondary educators in these content areas thus need to determine how they will merge these 10 reading standards and 20 writing standards (19 when excluding the narrative writing standard) with their content-area standards. Conclusion: these educators will now be responsible for *more* standards in their respective instructional programs than they were before. In the next chapter, I will share how educators in these content areas have been successfully prioritizing the 6–12 literacy standards.

| FIGURE 1.3 | Common Core State Standards—Literacy Standards to Emphasize in History/ Social Studies, Science, Technical Subjects, and Interdisciplinary Writing |

Grade Bands	History/ Social Studies	Science and Technology	Interdisciplinary Writing
Grades 6–8	10	10	20
Grades 9–10	10	10	20
Grades 11–12	10	10	19

Note: These literacy standards are not intended to replace existing content standards in those areas, but rather to *supplement* them.

| FIGURE 1.4 | Overview of the Common Core State Standards for Mathematics |

Overview of the Structure of the Common Core State Standards for Mathematics	
K–8	High School
Grade	Conceptual Category
Domain	Domain
Cluster	Cluster
Standards	Standards

Source: CCSSI, 2010.

Organization of the Common Core Math Standards

The K–8 Common Core State Standards for Mathematics (CCSSM) are grouped into three categories: *domains, clusters,* and *standards. Domains* are larger groups of related standards (geometry, measurement and data, operations and algebraic thinking, and so on). *Clusters,* within the domains, are groups of related standards. Standards from different domains and clusters may sometimes be closely related. *Standards,* within the clusters, define what students should understand and be able to do at each grade level. (See Figure 1.4.)

Figure 1.5 shows how these three components—Domain-Cluster-Standards—relate in a grade 3 example from the domain of Number and Operations in Base Ten.

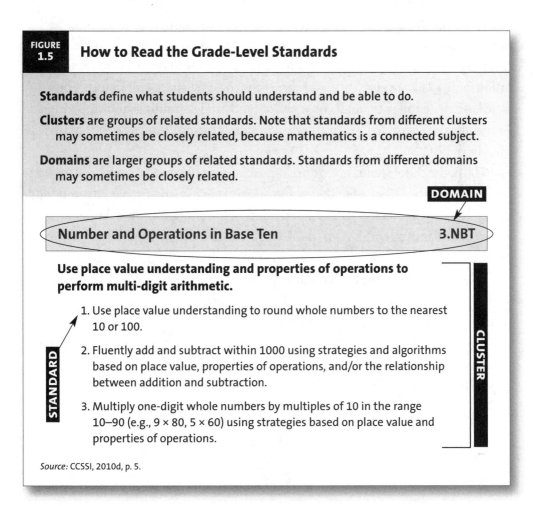

FIGURE 1.5 **How to Read the Grade-Level Standards**

Standards define what students should understand and be able to do.

Clusters are groups of related standards. Note that standards from different clusters may sometimes be closely related, because mathematics is a connected subject.

Domains are larger groups of related standards. Standards from different domains may sometimes be closely related.

DOMAIN

Number and Operations in Base Ten   **3.NBT**

Use place value understanding and properties of operations to perform multi-digit arithmetic.

1. Use place value understanding to round whole numbers to the nearest 10 or 100.

2. Fluently add and subtract within 1000 using strategies and algorithms based on place value, properties of operations, and/or the relationship between addition and subtraction.

3. Multiply one-digit whole numbers by multiples of 10 in the range 10–90 (e.g., 9 × 80, 5 × 60) using strategies based on place value and properties of operations.

STANDARD

CLUSTER

Source: CCSSI, 2010d, p. 5.

The K–5 CCSSM provide students with a solid foundation in whole numbers, addition, subtraction, multiplication, division, fractions, and decimals, with an emphasis on students experiencing "hands-on" learning in number concepts and operations, geometry, and algebra. They are organized into six domains: Counting and Cardinality (kindergarten only), Operations and Algebraic Thinking, Number and Operations in Base Ten (grades K–2 only), Number and Operations in Base Ten and Fractions (grades 3–5 only), Measurement and Data, and Geometry.

The grades 6–8 CCSSM are organized into six domains: Ratios and Proportional Relationships (grades 6–7 only), Functions (grade 8 only), The Number System, Expressions and Equations, Geometry, and Statistics and Probability.

The grades 6–8 standards are decidedly more "robust" and include a significantly greater emphasis on algebra than many grade 8 *state* standards require. For example, the preamble of the grade 8 CCSSM states: "In Grade 8, instructional time should focus on three critical areas: (1) formulating and reasoning about expressions and equations, including modeling an association in bivariate data with a linear equation, and solving linear equations and systems of linear equations; (2) grasping the concept of a function and using functions to describe quantitative relationships; (3) analyzing two- and three-dimensional space and figures using distance, angle, similarity, and congruence, and understanding and applying the Pythagorean Theorem" (http://www.corestandards.org/assets/CCSSI_Math%20 Standards.pdf).

The high school standards are organized into six conceptual categories—Number and Quantity, Algebra, Functions, Geometry, Statistics and Probability, and Modeling—which will then be assigned to math courses, either traditional or integrated, as proposed in Appendix A of the CCSSM. Modeling is emphasized across *all* conceptual categories.

Whereas nearly all of the *strands* in the English language arts CCSS are consistent in name across all grades, K–12, the *domains* in the math CCSS change names from one grade span to the next (K–5, 6–8) and in the high school *conceptual categories* (grades 9–12). Yet Figure 1.6 shows how these domains and conceptual categories are intentionally connected from one grade span to the next as *learning progressions* across the K–12 grades.

FIGURE 1.6 CCSS Progressions of Domains and Conceptual Categories

K	1	2	3	4	5	6	7	8	High School Conceptual Categories
Counting & Cardinality									
Number and Operations in Base Ten						Ratios and Proportional Relationships			Number and Quantity
			Number and Operations in Fractions			The Number System			
Operations and Algebraic Thinking						Expressions and Equations			Algebra
								Functions	Functions
Geometry									Geometry
Measurement and Data						Statistics and Probability			Statistics and Probability

The Standards for Mathematical Practice

Another major component of the Common Core State Standards for Mathematics are the Standards for Mathematical Practice (SMP). Applicable to every grade level and course, these eight standards describe *how* students are to engage with the mathematical content of each math domain and conceptual category. The SMP will be described in greater detail in Chapter Three.

Fewer Common Core State Standards in Mathematics

For years, studies of mathematics education comparing the United States to high-performing countries have led to the conclusion that the mathematics curriculum in the United States needs to be much more focused if we are ever to see a real improvement in student achievement. "The preamble for each grade level [of the CCSSM] begins with explicit descriptors of critical areas of focus for how best to use mathematics instructional time throughout the school year. *Focus, clarity,* and *specificity* [emphasis added] are foundational principles of the standards for mathematical content, and no more than four critical areas of focus are emphasized in any given grade level" (Wiggs, 2011, p. 49).

Figures 1.7 and 1.8 show the numerical breakdown of the math standards by domains for grades K–5 and 6–8. I have listed the numbers of these grade-specific standards within each domain in separate columns and then added the columns together to show the total number of math standards for each of these grades.

FIGURE 1.7	**Common Core State Standards—Grades K–5 Mathematics**

Grade Level	Counting & Cardinality	Operations & Algebraic Thinking	Number & Operations in Base Ten	Number & Operations in Fractions	Measure-ment & Data	Geometry	Totals
Kindergarten	10	5	1	—	3	6	25
Grade 1	—	8	9	—	4	3	24
Grade 2	—	4	11	—	10	3	28
Grade 3	—	9	3	9	14	2	37
Grade 4	—	5	6	14	9	3	37
Grade 5	—	3	9	14	10	4	40

FIGURE 1.8	**Common Core State Standards—Grades 6–8 Mathematics**

Grade Level	Ratio & Proportional Relationships	Number System	Expressions & Equations	Geometry	Statistics & Probability	Functions	Totals
Grade 6	7	15	12	4	9	—	47
Grade 7	7	11	6	6	13	—	43
Grade 8	—	2	13	12	4	5	36

At first glance, the totals do not seem nearly as daunting as the greater numbers of English language arts standards.

For example, in the grade 8 domain Functions, there are only five standards. That seems doable enough. Yet all five of those standards do not appear as single sentences (typically the way state standards are written) but rather as *full paragraph descriptions* of what students need to know and be able to do. One example is Standard NF.4, which reads as follows:

> NF.4. Construct a function to model a linear relationship between two quantities. Determine the rate of change and initial value of the function from a description of a relationship or from two (x, y) values, including reading these from a table or from a graph. Interpret the rate of change and initial value of a linear function in terms of the situation it models, and in terms of its graph or a table of values.

In the Number and Operations in Fractions domain for grade 5, there are only seven standards. Yet three of those seven standards each list two to three additional sub-points beneath them, providing further detail of what students need to know and be able to do relative to the main standard. This brings the total number of standards for that domain to fourteen. Here is one of those standards with its two sub-points.

> NF.5. Interpret multiplication as scaling (resizing), by:
>
> a. Comparing the size of a product to the size of one factor on the basis of the size of the other factor, without performing the indicated multiplication.
>
> b. Explaining why multiplying a given number by a fraction greater than 1 results in a product greater than the given number (recognizing multiplication by whole numbers greater than 1 as a familiar case); explaining why multiplying a given number by a fraction less than 1 results in a product smaller than the given number; and relating the principle of fraction equivalence a/b = (n x a) / (n x b) to the effect of multiplying a/b by 1.

Even though there is essentially only *one* connected mathematical idea represented in the grade 8 paragraph-length example and the grade 5 main standard with accompanying sub-points, the density of the content will prove formidable for educators to teach and for students to learn, both conceptually and procedurally.

Figure 1.9 shows the total number of standards across all conceptual categories that high school students must learn throughout three to four years of high school math courses. The second column lists the number of *modeling* standards found in each conceptual category. When added together, these numbers represent a steep learning curve that students (and teachers) must face. And the third column shows the 45 advanced course work standards (designated with a plus [+] symbol in the standards) that will prepare students for STEM (science, technology, engineering, or mathematics) careers.

Even though all of these figures showcase the total *numbers* of math standards, the issue of whether or not to prioritize the CCSSM should never be reduced simply to a "numbers game." The majority, if not all, of these standards represent a significant *increase in rigor* that will require much more instructional time and more learning opportunities in order for students to fully grasp them—conceptually, procedurally, and through application. Such standards should be identified as *priorities*, even if the total quantity of grade- or course-specific standards is not that large.

FIGURE 1.9	**Number of CCR and Advanced Course Work Standards**

CCSS Conceptual Category	Number of CCR Standards	Number of Modeling Standards (*)	Number of Advanced Course Work Standards (+)
Number and Quantity	9	3	18
Algebra	23	8	4
Functions	22	12	8
Geometry	37	6	6
Statistics and Probability	22	31 (all)	9
Modeling	Throughout all categories		
Total	**113**	**60**	**45**

Note that within the "Functions" conceptual category several standards include both CCR and advanced course work standards (for example 1a and 1b+).*

Are All Standards Equal? Is There Enough Time?

I wish to point out that the ideas presented in this book are not intended in any way to undermine the diligent and thoughtful work that has gone into the determination of the Common Core State Standards or the commendable published documents that those efforts produced. When the CCSS authors sat down to determine their respective content-area standards, the end results represented the collective set of knowledge and skills that they believed all students in grades K–12 need to master in order to be fully ready for college and/or career. Certainly our educators, school system leaders, board of education members, and parents *ideally* would want all students in their own school, district, and state to know and be able to demonstrate proficiency of each and every one of these standards. The issue here is not whether students *should* learn all the concepts and skills embedded in the CCSS each school year, but whether or not this is a realistic and achievable goal.

When deciding for yourself whether or not it is justifiable to prioritize the Common Core State Standards in English language arts and mathematics, consider these two questions:

- Does each and every one of the Common Core State Standards in the elementary, middle, and high school grades need *equal instruction and assessment emphasis* in order for students to be ready for the standards at the next level of learning?

- Will the length of the school year—from the start of school until late winter/early spring testing begins—give teachers enough time to adequately teach, assess, reteach, and reassess their students on *all* of the CCSS for their grade or course?

If the answer to either of these two questions is "*no*," then it only makes sense to consider prioritizing the Common Core.

How to Prioritize?

This then begs the question: *How* are the Common Core standards to be prioritized? For years, educators and leaders who have attended my Priority Standards workshops across the United States have resoundingly agreed that not all *state* standards are equal in importance. I typically posed the following question to the more experienced educators in the audience:

"Who among you has *ever* in one year been able to teach and assess all
the state standards for which you are responsible?"

No hands would go up; laughter would rise in the room instead.

I then asked these veteran educators, "So how do you decide which standards are
the most important ones to teach when you realize there is no way to teach all of
them effectively in the time you have?"

They answered, "We pick and choose!"

"Based on what?" I asked.

They called out a variety of responses, such as the following:

"What I like to teach."

"What I have materials for."

"What's on the test."

"What students need to know next year."

This invariably sparked animated table discussions. I would wait a few moments
for the talk to subside and then ask a leading question to make my point:

"But are all of you using the *same* selection criteria?"

The response was a mixture of laughter and groans. Everyone knew the answer
to *that* question: "No!"

Left to their own professional *opinions* when faced with the task of narrowing a
voluminous number of student learning outcomes, educators naturally "pick and
choose" those they know and like best, the ones for which they have materials and
lesson plans or activities, and those most likely to appear on state tests. But without
the benefit of *specific criteria* for prioritization, everyone understandably makes selections different from their colleagues, and then they wonder or lament why students come to them each year with a very diverse background of prior learning.

The Common Core standards differ from state standards in that *all* of them are
indeed important and interdependent. This leads to the central question: Which
standards will require a *greater degree of emphasis*? To thoughtfully prioritize either
the state standards *or* the Common Core, educators and leaders need to reference a
set of selection criteria that is both objective and effective. In the next two chapters,
I will present the established criteria for prioritizing the Common Core in English
language arts and mathematics, respectively.

Persistent Misconception #1

The most persistent misconception I have encountered over the last twelve plus years is the belief that prioritizing the standards is synonymous with *eliminating* certain standards in favor of others. Nothing could be further from the truth. All standards must be taught and assessed, and retaught and reassessed!

Identifying Priority Standards does not relieve teachers of the responsibility for teaching *all* the standards in the grade level or curricular area they have been assigned to teach. What is necessary is to make this important distinction—*which* standards require greater emphasis for student understanding, and which ones can be taught and assessed with *less* emphasis? The word "priority" infers by definition that there are *other* standards students need to learn. I refer to these other standards as *supporting standards.*

Supporting standards, as defined in the Introduction, are those standards that *support, connect to, or enhance* the Priority Standards. They are taught *within the context* of the priorities and often serve as instructional scaffolds, but they do not receive the *same* degree of instruction and assessment emphasis.

For example, here are two CCSS in English language arts from the grade 5 Informational Text reading strand. The first standard is bolded to indicate that it is a Priority Standard. The second standard is a supporting standard; it *supports, connects to, and enhances* the first, but most educators and leaders agree that it does not carry an *equal weight of instructional importance.*

> **CC.5.R.I.3. Explain the relationships or interactions between two or more individuals, events, ideas, or concepts in a historical, scientific, or technical text based on specific information in the text.**

> CC.5.R.I.1. Quote accurately from a text when explaining what the text says explicitly and when drawing inferences from the text.

Certainly there is value in students quoting accurately when providing explicit explanations and drawing inferences from a given text. Students should be able to cite quotations that *support, connect to, and enhance* their explanations of relationships or interactions as specified in the bolded standard above it. However, if there is not sufficient instructional time to emphasize both of these standards equally, then the educator must decide which of the two standards will *serve students the most.*

A metaphor I frequently use to illustrate the interdependence of Priority Standards and supporting standards is that of a fence made of both posts and rails. Like fence *posts*, Priority Standards provide curricular focus in which teachers need to "dig deeper" and assure student competency. Like fence *rails*, supporting standards are curricular standards that *connect to and support* the Priority Standards. Without both the posts and the rails, there can be no fence.

To further clarify the fence metaphor, consider a mathematical example that readers of *Power Standards* (Ainsworth, 2003a) may remember—the relative importance of two geometric shapes: the rectangle and the rhombus. In my own first year as an elementary math teacher, I struggled to give reasonably equal time and attention to *all* geometric shapes (the coverage approach to instruction). As a result, my students rarely received enough time and practice in finding the area of any one geometric shape to become really proficient at that skill.

In my second year of teaching, I thought it was more important for all students to really understood how to find the area of a rectangle rather than try and rush them through finding the area of all the other shapes (i.e., rhombus, parallelogram, trapezoid, and so on), so I spent much less time teaching those.

It finally dawned on me that if students really understood *conceptually and procedurally* how to find the area of a rectangle, I could then show them how to also apply that understanding to determine the area of a rhombus, trapezoid, or parallelogram—even though these other geometric shapes did not receive the same amount of instruction and hands-on practice as students had had with the rectangle.

In reference to the fence metaphor, the rectangle was decidedly a fence *post*, and the rhombus a fence *rail*.

Persistent Misconception #2

The other erroneous notion is that prioritizing the standards means "dumbing down" or lowering to the minimum what we expect students to learn and how we expect educators to teach. Priority Standards in past years were often those standards most heavily represented on state tests. As an unfortunate result, classroom instruction and assessments were often *reduced* to only those tested standards and their corresponding lower levels of cognitive rigor—often less than what the standards themselves required.

Prioritizing the standards has nothing whatsoever to do with "lowering the bar," and everything to do with *focus*. It is about "less" being *more*. This benefit will become increasingly evident as educators fully grasp what students will be required to know and do on the PARCC and SBAC national assessments in 2014/15. By focusing on those standards identified as the *most rigorous—not foundational,* as was often the case when "powering" state standards—they will be in a much stronger position to prepare their students for the challenge of these new exams.

Careful selection of a *subset* of rigorous, grade-specific and course-specific standards that are deemed essential for students to know and be able to do is only the "what." From there, educators must then teach these fewer numbers of standards for *depth of understanding, not coverage of content,* by enriching, expanding, and building upon foundational concepts and skills that students need in order to understand and apply more complex concepts and skills. It is important to note that Priority Standards actually make it possible for educators to be *more* creative and use *more* of their expertise because they are not continually "running on the standards treadmill," trying in vain to get everything in.

No Breaking the Learning Progressions!

Never an issue when prioritizing *state* standards, there is one occasional pushback I hear about prioritizing the Common Core: Regardless of the numbers of standards, the CCSS should *not* be prioritized since every standard is linked to a College and Career Readiness standard and is necessary for students to "master" in order to be ready to encounter the standards at the next level of learning. And because the CCSS have been carefully organized into *learning progressions,* the idea of prioritizing seems to violate this organizational structure. Let me be clear: It is critically important to emphasize to groups of educators that gather to prioritize the CCSS that this process does not "break" or violate the vertical learning progressions intentionally built into the fabric of the CCSS. We respect and maintain fidelity to the integrity of these spiraled standards. In the vertical alignment step of the prioritizing process, participating educators and leaders carefully look to see that those learning progressions do indeed remain intact and connected from one grade to the next, K–12.

To Postpone Prioritization—Or Not

School districts located in states that have adopted—but not yet prioritized—the Common Core State Standards may want to inquire whether or not there are statewide or regional plans to do this work. Even though the process of prioritizing and vertically aligning all of the CCSS in English language arts and math can be accomplished in approximately two to three days, it still requires a great deal of thought and work by many people. If there are such statewide or regional plans in place to soon prioritize the CCSS for the benefit of member districts, it certainly makes sense for an individual school district to wait for those products.

However, those school systems that are unsure as to when, or if, their state or region intends to prioritize the Common Core State Standards should proceed in prioritizing the CCSS on their own, or with partnering districts, as soon as possible. The benefits to doing so outweigh any benefits of delay. The numerous groups of educators and leaders across the country that I have led through the prioritizing process have all found tremendous value in being directly involved in this highly collaborative professional practice.

The following comment from one seminar participant echoes what many others have said: "This process required all of us here to deeply examine the wording and meaning of the Common Core. I had generally read through them prior to the seminar, but now I deeply understand exactly what these new standards will require of me in terms of both instruction and assessment. Had I been handed a set of Priority CCSS selected by others, I wouldn't have had the understanding that I do now of what they really mean."

Should the CCSS be prioritized by your state or region after your own district prioritization work is completed, you will already have had a firsthand experience with the process and be in a strong position to closely compare, contrast, and evaluate the state or regional selections with your own.

Because student achievement data from state exams have always been used to help determine the state Priority Standards, some may rightly question whether or not they should wait to prioritize the CCSS until they know more about the new standardized tests now being developed, field-tested, and revised by PARCC and SBAC. Both of these assessment consortia are regularly providing important information and updates regarding the content, rigor, and requirements of their respective assessments. Even though complete samples of the actual test items for every grade, 3 through 11, are not yet available on the respective Web sites, prototypes of sample items for representative grade levels are. Groups of educators and leaders should have access to the latest information regarding these new assessments as they select their Priority CCSS. This information clearly forecasts what students will be expected to know and do and can thus inform the Priority Standards selection process.

From a practical standpoint, it makes more sense to prioritize the Common Core now rather than wait until sometime in the future. Through this process, educators (and by extension, their students) will "get to know" the CCSS sooner rather than later. They will be in a much stronger position to make adjustments or changes to their prioritized selections as more information about the new assessments becomes available. It will be much easier and require less time to revisit and revise their Priority Standards than to wait to begin the whole endeavor from scratch when the pressure of impending new tests is weighing heavily on everyone.

To sum up, one of the greatest benefits to identifying Priority Standards is that they counteract the long-standing "coverage" approach to teaching student learning outcomes. Prioritized Common Core standards will provide educators with a sharp and consistent focus for *in-depth* instruction and related assessment. They will provide *students* with multiple opportunities to learn those standards throughout the school year as opposed to a one-time instructional exposure to them.

The next two chapters describe *how* to prioritize the Common Core—in English language arts and in mathematics, respectively. It will be helpful to read *both* chapters, even if your particular interest is in one content area versus the other. Not all of the information presented in Chapter Two repeats in Chapter Three. Together, the two chapters will provide you with a broader and deeper understanding of the entire process and assist you in prioritizing either content area of the CCSS.

READER'S ASSIGNMENT

1. Conduct a *needs assessment* with regard to prioritizing the Common Core:

   • Do you have the internal district capacity, including personnel and budget, to do this work on your own? If not, would it be a more effective use of resources (time, personnel, money) to partner with one or more neighboring districts to accomplish this?

   • Should you start with English language arts or math, or prioritize both content areas simultaneously?

   • Who will prioritize the 6–12 literacy standards? Secondary content-area supervisors with lead teachers? Interdisciplinary department groups together or separately by content areas? Will your secondary English teachers review the documents and provide input?

   • Do you know which, if any, of your state's current standards have been added to the CCSS? These will need to be prioritized *as part of* the Common Core for your state. (Note: Keep current regarding your own state's actions concerning this. One large state initially added its own standards to the Common Core and then recently decided to remove them, a change that many in the state were not aware of.)

2. Evaluate your current situation with regard to prioritizing existing *state* standards:

   • In which other content areas (science, history/social studies, visual and performing arts, P.E., etc.) do you have district-prioritized *state* standards already identified?

   • How long ago did you do this work? Do those selections need to be reviewed and possibly updated?

3. Develop an *action plan* for prioritizing the Common Core and/or existing state standards in one or more content areas using the following table as a guide. Note that this full chart is designed for use with the Rigorous Curriculum Design (2010) process for creating units of study aligned to the CCSS. The first foundational step of that process is to prioritize the Common Core. For purposes here, use the column headings as guidelines for developing your Priority Standards Action Plan.

Rigorous Curriculum Design Action Plan

Components	What?		When?	Who?	How Do We Get There?		How Do We Know?	
	Current State (What do we have in place now?)	Desired State (Where do we want to be?)	Time Frame (When do we want to get there?)	Lead/ Participants	Professional Development Provider & Time Frame	Needed Resources	Outcomes Artifacts & Due Dates	Monitoring Who? When?
Part II: Foundations								
Prioritize the Standards								
Name Units & Assign Standards								
Pacing Calendar								
Construct Unit Planning Organizer								
Part III: Unit Design								
Select Unit/Match Standards								
"Unwrapping" Priority Standards								
Graphic Organizer with Bloom's/DOK								
Big Ideas, Essential Questions								
Pre-/Post- Assessments								
Progress- Monitor Checks								
Engaging Learning Experiences								
High-Impact Instructional Strategies								
Detail the Units								
Weekly/Daily Planners								

CHAPTER TWO

How to Prioritize the English Language Arts and Literacy Common Core

In the absence of an agreed-upon set of criteria for prioritizing the Common Core, educators will, out of necessity, make up their own. Whether those criteria are implicitly understood or explicitly defined, the following question is uppermost in educators' minds as they consider which standards to emphasize the most:

> *"What knowledge and skills must I impart to my students <u>this</u> year so that they will enter <u>next</u> year's class with confidence and a readiness for success?"*

This question is what motivates educators to frequently say to their students, "Now *next* year, you are going to need to know and be able to do…" This is their way of forecasting for their students the importance of what they are *currently* learning as a preparation for the future, while simultaneously using that same criterion to emphasize certain standards over others in their instructional planning.

Priority Standards Selection Criteria

Priority Standards are collaboratively decided, so there is an absolute need for *objective* selection criteria. Douglas B. Reeves established the criteria for "powering" the standards in the late 1990s, and they have been used successfully for this purpose ever since. These criteria are:

- *Endurance* (lasting beyond one grade or course; concepts and skills needed in life). Will proficiency of this standard provide students with the knowledge and skills that will be of value beyond the present? For example, proficiency in reading informational texts and

being able to write effectively for a variety of purposes will endure
throughout a student's academic career and work life.

• *Leverage* (crossover application *within* the content area and to other
content areas; i.e., interdisciplinary connections). For example,
proficiency in creating and interpreting graphs, diagrams, and charts
and then being able to make accurate inferences from them will help
students in math, science, social studies, language arts, and other
areas. The ability to write an analytical summary or a persuasive
essay will similarly help students in any academic discipline.

• *Readiness for the next level of learning* (prerequisite concepts and
skills students need to enter a new grade level or course of study).
Will proficiency of this standard provide students with the essential
knowledge and skills that are necessary for future success? One of the
most important structural features of the Common Core standards is
that they spiral vertically from grade to grade in *learning progressions*
to ensure this readiness for the next level.

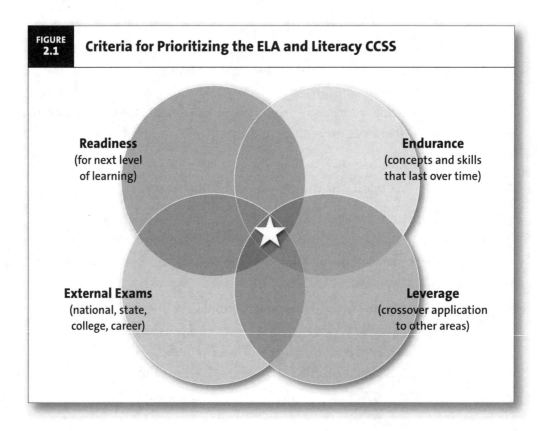

FIGURE 2.1

Criteria for Prioritizing the ELA and Literacy CCSS

Readiness
(for next level
of learning)

Endurance
(concepts and skills
that last over time)

External Exams
(national, state,
college, career)

Leverage
(crossover application
to other areas)

A fourth element must be added to these established selection criteria—the standardized tests, college entrance exams, and occupational competency exams students will need to prepare for.

Figure 2.1 represents these four key criteria for prioritizing the Common Core English language arts (ELA) and literacy standards.

The grade- or course-specific standards that meet *all four* of the above selection criteria will emerge as a clearly defined *subset* of the complete list of academic standards. As such, these Priority Standards will represent the essential knowledge and skills that *all* students must know and be able to do by the time they leave each grade, each grade span, each course, and high school. Because the fundamental tenet of the K–12 Common Core State Standards Initiative is to thoroughly *prepare* all students for both college and career, these carefully selected Priority Standards must serve that ultimate purpose.

Are These Criteria Equal in Importance?

I remember once discussing the Priority Standards identification criteria with a faculty of elementary educators. A fourth-grade teacher spoke up and said, "Certainly endurance, leverage, and readiness for the next grade level are important considerations for identifying Priority Standards, but the pressure we are under to produce improved state test scores is overshadowing everything else. Shouldn't that criterion carry more weight than the other three?"

On a large piece of chart paper, I quickly drew a quadruple Venn diagram, similar to the one in Figure 2.1. But I intentionally made the External Exams circle much larger than the other three.

Then I replied, "This circle is almost certain to be the continuing focus in American education, but for the overall success of our students, isn't it vitally important that we keep in mind what they will need for success in their remaining years of K–12 education, in college and career, and in life itself? *Learning that endures* should be an instructional goal that we never lose sight of. If we identify and concentrate on the standards that reflect the criteria in the other three circles (Endurance, Leverage, Readiness), isn't it likely that we will be effectively preparing students to also do well on standardized tests?"

The criteria of endurance, leverage, and readiness for the next level of learning are perfect for helping educators fulfill the promise of the Common Core—ensuring that all students are college and career ready by the end of high school. Inevitably, the fourth criterion (external exams) is now coming into prominent focus as new information, along with prototypes of sample items, continue to be released from the PARCC and SBAC assessment consortia.

SBAC and PARCC Test Specifications

When the PARCC and SBAC assessments officially replace existing state exams in 2014/15, these assessments will likely influence the decision of whether or not to revise the initial Priority Standards selections. Until then, my recommendation is to become familiar with the specific references both consortia are making about emphasizing certain CCSS over others—in both English language arts and mathematics. For example, the SBAC Content Specifications (http://www.smarterbalanced .org/smarter-balanced-assessments/) state: "Prioritization criteria for selecting standards (or parts of standards) to be assessed at the end of each grade level included this explanation: Content identified in the CCSS document as having greater emphasis at different grade levels was given the highest priority." Information pertinent to prioritizing the CCSS in English language arts can be found throughout the document. (Specific SBAC criteria for prioritizing the math CCSS will be provided in the next chapter.)

The PARCC Model Content Frameworks (http://www.parcconline.org/parcc -model-content-frameworks/) also provide guidance for emphasizing certain standards over others. For example, in English language arts "two standards are always in play—whether they be reading or writing items, selected-response or constructed-response items on any one of the four components of PARCC. They are: Reading Standard One (Use of Evidence) and Reading Standard Ten (Complex Texts)." Certainly these two standards need to be prominently in focus when prioritizing the CCSS. Other guidelines for prioritizing appear throughout the Model Content Frameworks. (Specific PARCC criteria for prioritizing the math CCSS will be provided in the next chapter.)

K–12 Publishers' Criteria

The Publishers' Criteria for the Common Core State Standards in English Language Arts and Literacy for Grades K–12 "provide insights into what the lead CCSS authors felt was important to emphasize instructionally (e.g., conducting short research projects)." Written by Common Core authors, the Publishers' Criteria for ELA are presented in two separate documents: one for grades K–2 and the other for grades 3–12. These guiding documents are available on the Common Core Web site at http://www.corestandards.org/. Click on "Resources" on the navigation bar to access these important criteria.

My strong recommendation to groups that gather to prioritize the CCSS is that they have access to and study *all* of the documents showcased in this chapter with an eye to discerning the major themes, big ideas, concepts, and skills that are receiving the greatest emphasis. Almost certainly these areas of focus will translate into testable items on the SBAC and PARCC assessments. Use this information as another "lens" through which to look when prioritizing the Common Core, in English language arts and literacy, and in mathematics.

Determine the Most Rigorous Standards

Key point to remember: When considering whether to select one Common Core grade-level standard over another, carefully determine which one is the more *comprehensive* or *rigorous*—not the more foundational. When pondering which of two similar standards to select as a priority, educators will often say, "If students could do this one, then they would certainly be able to do this other one." One helpful way to identify the *supporting* standards is to see which ones can be subsumed into the more rigorous or comprehensive priorities. Many of the Common Core ELA standards within a particular strand are similar to one another. Educators determine which standards are the more rigorous, select those as the priorities, and then look for one or two other *supporting standards* that will serve as "instructional scaffolds," or prerequisites, to help students attain the more rigorous or comprehensive ones.

For example, in the Reading Literature strand, a group of upper elementary educators in West Hartford, Connecticut, selected as the priority:

RL.4.2. Determine a theme of a story, drama, or poem from details in the text; summarize the text.

They chose the following as the supporting standards that educators would use as instructional scaffolds to help students ultimately understand and demonstrate the more rigorous and comprehensive one:

RL.4.1. Refer to details and examples in a text when explaining what the text says explicitly and when drawing inferences from the text.

RL.4.5. Explain major differences between poems, drama, and prose, and refer to the structural elements of poems (e.g., verse, rhythm, meter) and drama (e.g., casts of characters, settings, descriptions, dialogue, stage directions) when writing or speaking about a text.

RL.4.7. Make connections between the text of a story or drama and a visual or oral presentation of the text, identifying where each version reflects specific descriptions and directions in the text.

To show these intentional connections between the Priority Standards and the supporting standards in their district Priority Standards published documents, they decided to *resequence* the standards within the strand (as the above example shows). They did not change any of the wording of the CCSS, only the position within the strand in which the standards appear. Their purpose in repositioning the standards in this way was to show the instructional connections between the Priority Standards and the supporting standards.

How Many Do We Choose?

A question seminar participants always ask as they are about to begin the prioritization process is: How many Priority Standards should we choose?

Based on his research of the numbers of *state* standards, presented in the Introduction, Robert Marzano (Sherer, 2001) advocated a reduction to approximately *one-third* the total number of grade- or course-specific state standards for a given content area. For years, this "one-third rule" has proved to be quite accurate when prioritizing state standards—particularly in mathematics. However, because this research was based on state standards and took place prior to the Common Core, this fractional guideline is not as applicable as it once was. In my own experience leading groups of educators and leaders through the process of prioritizing the CCSS in English language arts, participants are selecting from one-third to *one-half* of the total number of grade-specific standards in English language arts. In some strands they will select more priorities than in other strands—not one-half of *each* strand.

What If We Pick the "Wrong" Ones?

Often educators express concern that they may not be selecting the "right" standards as priorities. I reassure them by saying that these selections are not final; they will be revisited, reviewed, and revised as needed, not only by the present group of participants who are making the initial selections, but also with the feedback and input of their district colleagues who are not involved in the first part of the process (see Chapter Four). Also, since this process is taking place *with the same standards* in school systems across the country, districts for the first time will be able to compare and contrast their own Priority Standards selections with those of other districts in other states, and use that information to confirm or rethink their choices.

The Priority Standards are intended to be *living, in-process* documents that lend themselves to change as new information becomes available from SBAC and PARCC and as educators instruct and assess their students on the Common Core and then reflect on the results.

A Practice in Prioritizing

Before beginning the actual prioritization of the ELA standards, it is helpful to first provide participants with a "warm-up" activity. Not only does this activity set the stage for the work to come; it also makes participants aware that they should not anticipate or expect easy agreement. Ongoing discussions and changes to initial selections are inherent in the overall process.

I always recommend starting with the Informational Text strand, and the following exercise in prioritizing the grade 6 standards in that strand is a great introduction, especially when working with a K–12 group.

Prioritizing the Common Core:
A Practice Activity in English Language Arts

Priority Standards represent a carefully selected subset of the total list of the grade-specific and course-specific standards within each content area. This subset represents what students must know and be able to do *by the end of each school year* in order to be prepared to enter the next grade level or course (Ainsworth, *Rigorous Curriculum Design*, 2010, pp. 39–40).

Priority Standards must meet these selection criteria: endurance, leverage, and a readiness or prerequisite for the next level of learning (Reeves, *Accountability in Action*, 2004, and *Making Standards Work*, 1997–2004). They should also reflect those concepts and skills likely to be most emphasized on state or national assessments, and on college and career entrance exams (grades 9–12).

Directions:

Please identify **four** of the following ten Common Core State Standards in the Informational Text strand using these Priority Standards selection criteria:

• *Endurance* (lasting beyond one grade or course; concepts and skills needed in life)

• *Leverage* (crossover application *within* the content area and to other content areas; i.e., interdisciplinary connections)

• *Readiness for the next level of learning* (prerequisite concepts and skills students need to enter a new grade level or course of study)

• *External Exams* (state and national, college and career entrance; SBAC and PARCC information relative to prioritization).

Common Core State Standards—
Grade 6 Reading Standards for Informational Text (RI):

_____ RI.6.1. Cite textual evidence to support analysis of what the text says explicitly as well as inferences drawn from the text.

_____ RI.6.2. Determine a central idea of a text and how it is conveyed through particular details; provide a summary of the text distinct from personal opinions or judgments.

_____ RI.6.3. Analyze in detail how a key individual, event, or idea is introduced, illustrated, and elaborated in a text (e.g., through examples or anecdotes).

_____ RI.6.4. Determine the meaning of words and phrases as they are used in a text, including figurative, connotative, and technical meaning.

_____ RI.6.5. Analyze how a particular sentence, paragraph, chapter, or section fits into the overall structure of a text and contributes to the development of the ideas.

_____ RI.6.6. Determine an author's point of view or purpose in a text and explain how it is conveyed in the text.

_____ RI.6.7. Integrate information presented in different media or formats (e.g., visually, quantitatively) as well as in words to develop a coherent understanding of a topic or issue.

_____ RI.6.8. Trace and evaluate the argument and specific claims in a text, distinguishing claims that are supported by reasons and evidence from claims that are not.

_____ RI.6.9. Compare and contrast one author's presentation of events with that of another (e.g., a memoir written by and a biography on the same person).

_____ RI.6.10. By the end of the year, read and comprehend literary non-fiction in the grades 6–8 text complexity band proficiently, with scaffolding as needed at the high end of the range.

I first ask participants to carefully read on their own the listed standards. Next, while referring to the prioritization criteria, they independently make their initial selections. Then I ask them to compare/contrast their choices with those of their table colleagues, noting where they agree and disagree, and try to agree on four. When all groups are finished, a spokesperson for each of the table groups shares out with the large group their four selections along with a short summary of their discussions, including how (and if) they reached consensus. As each group reports out their top four choices, I tally them on a large piece of poster paper numbered one through ten. Everyone can see which standards are emerging as the priorities for that particular grade, which ones are marginal and will need further discussion, and which ones are receiving the fewest votes.

I am particularly interested in the number of votes Standard 10 receives.

Reading Standard 10—An Overarching Goal Statement

In grades 2 through 12, Standard 10 of the Common Core reading standards in the strands of Literature and Informational Text specifies the range of reading and level of text complexity that students must be able to demonstrate by the end of the academic year. The wording of Standard 10 in both strands is essentially the same in each grade. Here are two samples:

> **Literature:** By the end of the year, read and comprehend literature, including stories, dramas, and poetry, at the high end of the grades 4–5 text complexity band independently and proficiently.

> **Informational Text:** By the end of the year, read and comprehend literary nonfiction in the grades 6–8 text complexity band proficiently, with scaffolding as needed at the high end of the range.

In March 2011, I was working with a large group of educators and leaders in Ashland, Oregon. They had gathered for a one-day understanding and application of the process of prioritizing the Common Core. Several participants in the K–12 audience had selected Standard 10 as a priority. Two individuals brought it to everyone's attention that because this particular standard expects students to be able to proficiently read both literary and informational texts at the *high end of the grade-level range*, it carries more weight and influence than a single Priority Standard; it applies to *all* of the standards within the two strands.

Everyone in the room had a spontaneous "aha" moment, and as a result, it was agreed that Standard 10 would receive a new classification as an *Overarching Goal Statement*. It would be placed at the top of the strand to emphasize its importance and its direct impact/influence on the nine standards listed below it.

Since that time, I have facilitated groups of educators and leaders from coast to coast in coming to this same awareness, followed by two key questions to enable them to formulate their own district position on the matter:

1. If you do *not* choose to emphasize Standard 10 as an Overarching Goal Statement, what message does this send to everyone? (Answer: Students can demonstrate proficiency in Standards 1–9, but they can do so using *below-grade-level* reading texts.)

2. If you *do* choose to emphasize Standard 10 as an Overarching Goal Statement, what message does this send to everyone? (Answer: We expect our students to become proficient at Standards 1–9, and they must be doing so while reading *grade-level* texts—at the high end of the text complexity range.)

To date, every group of educators and leaders has selected the *second* answer choice—and has voiced the idea of regarding *Writing* Standard 10 in the same way. Not only is that answer in keeping with the rigorous expectations of the Common Core, it also shines a bright light on the challenges that educators will face in striving to carry out the instructional implications of that choice.

The Six-Step Prioritization Process at a Glance

Figure 2.2 provides a quick overview of the six-step process for prioritizing the Common Core. This chapter describes Steps 1–4 as applied to English language arts and literacy. The next chapter applies these same four steps to mathematics, followed by an explanation of Steps 5 and 6 in the following chapter. Chapter Eleven provides a succinct summary of each step that can be used to familiarize others who were not directly involved in the initial selection of the Priority Standards.

FIGURE
2.2
Priority Standards at a Glance

Step 1: Make initial selections; Reach initial consensus.

Step 2: Reference SBAC Content Specifications and/or PARCC Model Content Frameworks and the ELA K–12 Publishers' Criteria; Make changes as needed.

Step 3: Chart selections for each grade.

Step 4: Vertically align Priority Standards K–12; Resolve uncertainties; Reach group consensus.

Step 5: Acquire feedback from all sites.

Step 6: Revise, publish, and distribute.

Preliminary Preparation

Organize by Grade-Span Groups and Getting Started

When working with a K–12 group, I ask participants to seat themselves in one of four grade-span groups: K–2, 3–5, 6–8, or 9–12. We then discuss which ELA strand they would like to prioritize first. Because of the increased focus on informational text in the Common Core, we invariably choose to begin the process with the Informational Text strand.

Within each grade-span group, members next choose <u>one</u> of the grades in which to begin, typically the first grade in the grade span (K, 3, 6, or 9). If individual grade-span groups are large, participants can subdivide into individual grade-level teams. The groups prepare to begin by locating in the CCSS documents the Informational Text strand for their targeted starting grade.

Review Priority Standards Identification Criteria

I remind participants to continually keep in mind the selection criteria for prioritizing:

- Endurance

- Leverage

- Readiness for the next level of learning

- Most rigorous or comprehensive

- "Fence posts" (described in Chapter One)

Step One: Make Initial Selections

Read and Select Independently

Now I ask the groups for a few minutes of silence during which each person is to in-dependently read the nine grade-specific standards for that strand (Standard 10 has already been identified as an Overarching Goal Statement during the warm-up ac-tivity) and quickly mark *no more than four or five* that they consider to be absolutely essential for student success—the priorities. I ask them to please wait to talk to col-leagues sitting next to them until after everyone has finished this first task.

"Just check the ones you think students must know and be able to do, the ones that you consider to be the most rigorous or comprehensive. As you find ones that you're not sure about, mark them with a question mark and continue on down the list. Ready? Please begin."

The group sets to work, and the room is silent as people engage in the task. When five to seven minutes have elapsed, I call the group back together, even though all are not finished. I ask them, "Why am I giving you so little time for something so im-portant? Why not ten, fifteen, even twenty minutes to do this?"

Almost always the response is, "We'd end up with everything checked, and we'd be right back where we started, with too much!"

I reply, "And that's exactly the reason. The longer we think about each one, the more standards we mark, since the standards collectively represent a comprehen-sive list of the knowledge and skills we want *all* students to learn in a deep and mean-ingful way. But to first pick out those most rigorous standards that 'hit you at the gut level,' the initial time limitation helps in doing this."

Reaching Initial Consensus

The goal of this first discussion is to *reach an initial consensus* of what the Priority Standards in the Informational Text strand should be for each targeted grade. I share with everyone a key guideline I learned years ago from Dr. Reeves when he addressed the challenge of groups striving to reach a consensus: "Perfection is not an option here, so forget the myth of 100 percent agreement—aim instead for a 'super-majority' consensus of eighty percent or so agreement."

Because professional educators have sound reasons for considering different points of view from their colleagues, I also mention an effective focus question that I once heard from Heidi Hayes Jacobs: "What *can* we agree on that all of our students need to know and be able to do by the end of each grade and course?" And then I add: "While you strive to actively listen to each other's varying points of view, keep this in mind as the underlying goal of the work—what *students* need for success, not what we prefer to teach!"

The other important point I bring out to participants is that it is okay to change their minds. In later steps of the process, their preliminary selections will be reconsidered and either confirmed or rejected as priorities. In particular, this happens during Step 2 when groups reference information related to prioritizing the CCSS from the SBAC and PARCC assessment consortia, and especially in Step 4 when the entire K–12 group discusses the vertical alignment of selections that begins in kindergarten and culminates in grade 12.

Let the Collaboration Begin!

After setting this stage for collaboration, I announce to everyone, "Now you're ready to talk in depth with your colleagues at the table. Share the standards that you marked with each other, and note where you agree, where you disagree, and where you're not sure. Talk about the ones you flagged with a question mark. If one of your colleagues does not have a standard marked that you consider a priority, did s/he see that particular one as being a *supporting* standard to a different priority? The goal is to reach an initial consensus at your table of what the four or five Informational Text Priority Standards should be for the particular grade you started with."

The room immediately comes alive with animated conversation as participants discuss their choices and note similarities and differences. While this discussion is taking place, I walk around the room and listen in on the conversations. Often, what I hear is easy agreement on two or three standards and "split votes" on the others. When there is a difference of opinion, it usually has to do with an individual's own interpretation of what a particular standard means.

One educator will say to another, "I didn't pick that standard because I saw it incorporated into this other one." In other words, through discussion, what initially appeared as disagreement was, in fact, merely a different interpretation. In general, educators usually agree on what they deem important for students to learn. They are able to justify their choices with logic and from experience; and where they cannot agree, they discuss their differing positions. If they are still unable to reach initial consensus, they flag the standard(s) in question for later discussion with the larger K–12 group. In this way, the process can keep moving forward, rather than having it get bogged down if consensus is not quickly achieved.

When the grade-span groups (K–2, 3–5, 6–8, and 9–12) have come to an initial consensus about the Priority Standards for *one* grade in their grade span, I ask them to repeat the same process with the *other* grades in the grade span. (Large groups of educators within *each* grade span will be completing this initial prioritizing sooner since they will be subdivided into grade-level groups and only looking at *one* grade within the grade span rather than all three.) After the grade-span groups all complete these tasks, I bring them back together as a K–12 group to provide directions for Step 2.

Step Two: Look for Connections to PARCC or SBAC Assessments

Whenever groups of educators and leaders have prioritized *state* standards, particularly those in state-tested content areas (reading, writing, math, and science), they always checked their initial selections of Priority Standards against their student achievement data to see if the standards they are identifying as priorities are the same ones that are most heavily emphasized on state exams.

Even though the current standardized tests in most of the 46 states are likely to continue to be administered to students until the PARCC and SBAC assessments replace those exams in 2014/15, implementation of the Common Core in all participating states is well underway. (Some states and state agencies, such as Kentucky and Washington, D.C., respectively, have already modified their standardized tests to include items based on the Common Core.) As a result, educators are finding themselves in the awkward position of being expected to teach new standards that do not align well to existing state tests. The understandable thinking of educators in these states is that because the Common Core State Standards are *more rigorous* than existing state standards,* if they focus their instruction on the Common Core, then students will likely do better on the state test that is based on the less-rigorous state standards.

When prioritizing the CCSS, participants should be checking their initial selections against the available information from the PARCC Model Content Frameworks and/or the SBAC Content Specifications as to the stated points of emphasis in those documents, *and* against the K–12 Publishers' Criteria for English Language

---

*The Thomas B. Fordham Institute's ranking (2010) of state standards compared to CCSS showed that 34 states had standards inferior to the Common Core in English language arts, and 37 states in mathematics. However, certain states—California and Massachusetts, for example—had standards *more* rigorous than the CCSS, even though those states still chose to adopt the CCSS.

Arts and Literacy. However, at this early point in the prioritizing process, I often recommend postponement of this important external check in order to keep the initial selection of the priorities in all strands moving forward, relying for now on participants' collective expertise and professional judgment to make initial determinations of the Priority CCSS. Then, when ready to refer to the PARCC and/or SBAC information and view *sample questions* students will encounter on the new tests (visit www.smarterbalanced.org and/or www.parcconline.org), the groups can revisit their initial Priority Standards selections and make changes accordingly.

Step Three: Chart Selections for Each Grade

When the four grade-span groups have finished determining the Priority Standards for each of their respective grades, I ask them to chart their selections on large pieces of paper, one sheet per grade, with the following information:

- Grade level and name of strand (e.g., Grade 3 Informational Text)

- The Common Core coding with grade level, strand, and standard number (e.g., 5.RI.3)

- *Full text* of each selected Priority Standard (if the standard is lengthy, write only a synopsis or brief phrase that summarizes the content of the standard)

- Fractional count of Priority Standards and total number of standards in the strand (e.g., 4/10 or, in the case of the Reading Informational Text and Literature strands with Standard 10 now classified as an Overarching Goal Statement, 4/9) to ensure that groups are not selecting too many priorities (e.g., 8/10).

The grade-span groups then post their charts, in grade-level sequence from kindergarten to grade 12, side by side on a wall of the room. After all 13 charts* are posted for everyone to see, the groups are now ready to engage in the most dynamic step of the process: vertically aligning the K–12 Informational Text standards.

---

*I recommend four separate charts for grades 9–12, even though the Common Core presents the high school standards in two grade bands of 9–10 and 11–12. This will sharply focus the vertical discussion on *how* grades 10 and 12 will differ from grades 9 and 11, respectively, when the standards are the same in those two grade bands. There will be a total of 13 charts, assuming high school participants distinguish grade-specific Priority Standards for grades 9, 10, 11, and 12 from the *grade-band* standards of 9–10 and 11–12.

The Power of Vertical Alignment

During the initial selection of Priority Standards for each individual grade level, the conversations between and among participants always revolve around the key question, "What do students need to know and be able to do by the *end* of this particular school year or course of study in order to be successfully prepared to enter the *next* grade level or course of study?"

After the Priority Standards are identified for the separate grade levels, they must then be vertically aligned with the Priority Standards selected for the grade levels *above and below.* And this alignment must be seamlessly apparent from kindergarten through high school to ensure that the learning progressions carefully built into the design of the CCSS remain intact.

Step Four: Vertically Align Standards K–12

Share Out of Grade-Span Selections

The entire group of participants is now ready to come together and take an in-depth, collective look at the vertical "flow" of the Priority Standards selections from grade to grade, kindergarten through grade 12. Everyone knows they may raise questions about any group's selections in order to reach a K–12 agreement as to which standards are to be the priorities at each grade level. Often secondary educators pose thought-provoking questions and perspectives for elementary educators to consider, and vice versa.

"Please select one or more members from your grade-span group to stand next to each grade-level chart and provide for the entire K–12 group a brief narrative about the Priority Standards you selected for each of your grades. Share with us any issues or questions that came up while working through the process."

The K–2 grade-span group is first to report out to the entire group, beginning with their selections for kindergarten and followed by grades 1 and 2. Certain standards may be identified as priorities in all three grades, while others may appear in one or two grades only. Everyone looks for the connections between the priorities from one grade to the next in the K–2 grade span and asks clarifying questions of the spokesperson(s).

When the discussion of the K–2 selections is about to conclude, I ask the *3–5* grade-span team two questions:

"If students entering third grade were truly proficient in these
identified K–2 Priority Standards, would you be happy? (Heads nod
happily. The "readiness for next level of learning" is confirmed.)

"Is there anything else you would want your primary grade colleagues
to emphasize so that students are better prepared for grade three?"
(Usually no additional changes are requested, but if there are, the
teams discuss it and make adjustments accordingly.)

After this confirmation is complete, all participants highlight the identified K–2
Priority Standards on their own hard copy of the K–12 standards, and the 3–5 grade-
span team's spokesperson(s) step up to share their charted information, grade by
grade. The process repeats as it did with the K–2 grade span and then continues with
the remaining two grade-span groups, 6–8 and 9–12. In this way, the entire K–12
group "signs off" on the vertically aligned Informational Text Priority Standards for
each of the 13 grades.

Having led educators and leaders through the prioritization process of both state
standards and the Common Core for so many years, I am convinced that the greatest benefit occurs during the animated, thoughtful, and truly collaborative discussions that take place while the groups of participants are fully engaged in this fourth
step of the process. Here the whole group can view the full K–12 breadth of the
strand and decide together if the priorities in one grade will enable students to be
ready for the priorities in the next. Participants are continually looking at the charted
selections of the grades below and the grades above the current grade in focus, com-
menting, suggesting changes, or asking for further clarification whenever needed.
One great benefit to having so many "eyes" scrutinizing the lists is that sometimes
educators in other grade-span teams can be more objective in spotting a discrep-
ancy or need for revision that might otherwise go unnoticed by those who work
with those grade-specific standards each and every day.

Being professional educators with content-area expertise, participants may not
always agree with one another, but they "agree to disagree." To keep the discussion
moving, any time a group seems to be at an impasse over a particular standard, I
suggest they put a Post-It note on the chart by the standard in question and revisit
the issue later. This proves effective in resolving uncertainties, keeping the process
flowing, and in ultimately reaching consensus.

When the K–12 group finishes this first vertical alignment exercise in an hour or
sometimes less, there is a genuine sense of professional satisfaction. They have

produced a first draft of the K–12 Informational Text Priority Standards! After taking a break, everyone returns energized to repeat the same process with the next section of the Common Core ELA standards, usually the Literature strand.

Typically, groups will replicate the entire process as a full K–12 group for the first two or three strands. But then, as some teams are waiting for others to finish, they start selecting their priorities in the other strands not yet done. When this occurs, consider this time-saving hint for vertically aligning the remaining strands: Ask the early-finishing grade-span teams to vertically align their selections *within* their own individual grade span (K–2, 3–5, 6–8, or 9–12) so they can keep working and not have to wait while other groups finish. When all four grade-span teams are finished doing this, join together as a K–12 group to vertically align the selections that *bridge* the grade spans (grades 2 to 3, grades 5 to 6, and grades 8 to 9). This will save time and keep everyone purposefully involved—a much-appreciated benefit for busy educators, especially when everyone is very desirous of identifying and vertically aligning all of the CCSS within the total number of hours or days allotted for doing this important work.

Whether utilizing this time-saving idea or not, I highly recommend that the full K–12 group thoughtfully reviews and agrees upon the selections of *each and every grade* so as to confirm that the Priority Standards and their vertical alignment represent the collective agreement of all participants. Grade-span participants can also conduct "gallery walks" to view the charts of other grade spans and make note of any questions they have for later discussion with the whole group. Be flexible and encourage everyone to suggest other ways to ensure that this grade-by-grade review and confirmation of selections by all participants can effectively take place.

Keeping Intact the Learning Progressions of the Common Core

In assisting school systems in the development of curriculum maps, Heidi Hayes Jacobs urges educators to look for "gaps, overlaps, and omissions" to ensure that curriculum is not heavily repeated or inadvertently omitted from one grade to another (1997).

Whenever I have facilitated groups of educators and leaders vertically aligning *state* standards, it has been particularly helpful during this step to look for and identify those gaps, overlaps, and omissions—not only within one grade but especially across multiple grades. I ask participants to be on the alert for the following three "red flags" as they listen to each grade-span group's narrative:

- Is there a certain standard that needs to be emphasized in more than one grade that is *missing* from a particular grade's list (a *gap*)?

- Is there a certain standard that is being *redundantly emphasized* in three or four grades that could be thoroughly taught in only one grade or two and then maintained in subsequent grades (an *overlap*)?
- Is there a particular standard *completely missing* from two or more grades that will cause a serious "break" in the learning progressions (an *omission*)?

Although this last "red flag" often occurred with state standards, this is unlikely to be a factor with the Common Core. The authors of the Common Core were intentional in "spiraling" the standards from one grade to the next; these inherent learning progressions are meant to ensure that there are *no* gaps or omissions in the standards. Any apparent "overlaps" are not to be misconstrued as oversight redundancies, but rather are meant to emphasize the *increasing rigor and focus* of a particular standard from one grade to the next.

Vertically Aligning the Priority Standards

The case could be argued, therefore, that there is no need for educators and leaders to vertically align the CCSS—they are *already* vertically aligned. What seminar participants are doing in this step of the prioritizing process is making sure that there is a clear vertical pathway of the *Priority Standards* from one grade to the next and from one grade span to the next.

When the Common Core was rapidly being adopted by states in the second half of 2010, groups that assembled to prioritize the CCSS thought this vertical alignment step was almost unnecessary. Initially, they believed that all they needed to do to prioritize the CCSS was to select their priorities *for each strand* and then, because many of the standards of that strand appeared again and again from one grade to the next with increasing complexity and/or rigor (the spiraled learning progressions), whichever standards were selected as the priorities of the strand would be the same in *every* grade level.

Grade-span groups soon learned that this was not the correct approach. They realized that a certain standard within a particular strand that was identified as a priority in one, two, or even three grades was not necessarily a priority in *all* grades. In other words, that standard might be a priority in grade 6 and grade 7, for example, and then become a *supporting* standard in grade 8 because the educators believed there were *other* standards for that grade in that strand that needed greater emphasis.

According to the aims of the Common Core, students are to "master" a Priority Standard during a particular year of school. The following year, an educator will be sure to maintain and reinforce student understanding of that standard, but the *instructional emphasis* may out of necessity need to shift to another standard. That original standard, once a priority and now a support, will not be overlooked; it will be *reinforced* within the context of a different instructional emphasis. In this way, students will have a much greater likelihood of ultimately fulfilling the goal of the Common Core—all students learning *all* standards by the end of high school so as to be academically ready to enter college and/or career.

Prioritizing the 6–12 Literacy Standards for Science and History/Social Studies

As stated in the previous chapter, the authors of the Common Core regard literacy as a shared responsibility across all content areas. To this end, reading and writing standards for grades 6–12 history/social studies and science and technical subjects are a focal point of the CCSS. Again, these literacy standards are not intended to replace existing content standards in those areas, but rather to *supplement* them. Secondary educators in these content areas thus need to determine how they will emphasize these literacy standards *in tandem with* their content-area standards. (Reminder: K–5 literacy standards for history/social studies and science/technical subjects are embedded within the K–5 content strands.)

With the addition of literacy standards to their instructional "plate," secondary educators in these content areas are meeting in grades 6–12 teams to prioritize these 10 reading standards and 20 writing standards (19 in grades 11–12). Content-area groups I have worked with are identifying as priorities about *half* of these standards (5 in reading and 10 in writing). They are then comparing and contrasting their own content-area selections to determine where their literacy emphasis is the same and where it differs.

In the district of McMinnville, Oregon, the secondary science and history/social studies educators went one step further: they consulted with their secondary English language arts colleagues to receive feedback on their selections. Figure 2.3 shows the chart they drew on the whiteboard to compare and contrast the selections of priority literacy standards from the perspectives of their individual content areas.

This recommended cross-department collaboration will prove quite helpful in promoting interdisciplinary connections. The history/social studies educators, along with the science and technology educators, can confer with the English language

FIGURE 2.3 **Interdisciplinary Perspectives of 6–12 Literacy Priorities**

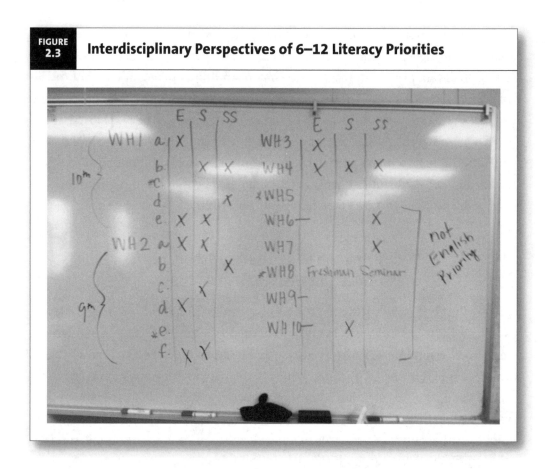

arts educators to look at the reading and writing standards and discuss which priority literacy standards to emphasize in their respective content-area courses.

Prioritizing the Common Core English language arts and literacy standards is a dynamic and doable process. It is a powerful way to help educators deeply understand the meaning of these standards and the implications they have for curriculum and assessment design, for instructional planning, and for helping students to ultimately achieve the "promise of the Common Core."

Prepare Grade-Span Summaries of the Process Followed

The final two steps of the Priority Standards process (how to involve *all* colleagues and then use their feedback to revise the initial selections) are described in Chapter Four. To help accomplish these eventual last steps, seminar participants can be asked to complete one additional task.

After teams select and vertically align the K–12 Priority Standards in *all* strands (or after *each* strand, if preferred), each grade-span group prepares for district coordinators a short summary of the process they followed for each strand (or domain in math). This summary should include, but is not limited to:

- How their group accomplished the task of prioritizing and vertically aligning the K–12 standards for each strand (each domain in mathematics)—a short explanation of their process

- Insights they gained during discussions and important points to remember

- Issues that arose and how they resolved them

- Advice or information for colleagues who were not part of the initial selection process.

This informational summary will prove very useful in promoting a sense of shared ownership of the Priority Standards drafts when showing them to their colleagues who were not part of the initial selection procedure.

READER'S ASSIGNMENT

Following the four-step process described in this chapter, organize your groups of educators and leaders to determine your own first draft of the Priority Standards for the K–12 English language arts CCSS and for the 6–12 literacy standards in history/social studies and science and technical subjects. Refer again to the section headings in this chapter to refresh your memory of the various tasks associated with each step. You may also wish to refer to Chapter Eleven for a more concise, step-by-step checklist to reference as you work through the process.

CHAPTER THREE

How to Prioritize the Mathematics Common Core

Introduced in Chapter One, the Common Core State Standards for Mathematics (CCSSM) include the Standards for Mathematical Content for grades K–8; the Standards for Mathematical Content for high school; and the eight Standards for Mathematical Practice (SMP), applicable K–12.

The Standards for Mathematical Content

The Standards for Mathematical Content, organized by domains in grades K–8 and by conceptual categories for high school math courses, balance and blend conceptual understanding with procedural understanding and application. Students who lack conceptual understanding of a math topic typically overrely on procedures. Without a strong knowledge base of mathematical understanding from which to begin, students are less likely to apply math to practical situations, think and reason mathematically, use technology as a tool to expedite their work, explain their thinking, and reflect on their process.

Charting a Pathway Through the Domains

Unlike English language arts, where the names of the strands remain the same from kindergarten through grade 12, the math domain names change from the elementary grades to the middle school grades to the high school conceptual categories.

However, in order for educators and leaders to see the mathematical "throughlines" of the standards from kindergarten through high school when they are prioritizing the grade- and course-specific standards, it is important to know the pathways of the various domains from one grade span to the next. Reprinted here from Chapter One, Figure 3.1 shows how these domains and conceptual categories connect between the three major grade spans (K–5, 6–8, and high school).

FIGURE 3.1	CCSS Progressions of Domains and Conceptual Categories

K	1	2	3	4	5	6	7	8	High School Conceptual Categories
Counting & Cardinality									
Number and Operations in Base Ten						Ratios and Proportional Relationships			Number and Quantity
			Number and Operations in Fractions			The Number System			
Operations and Algebraic Thinking						Expressions and Equations			Algebra
							Functions		Functions
Geometry									Geometry
Measurement and Data						Statistics and Probability			Statistics and Probability

Mathematics Learning Progressions

Simply defined, learning progressions are the "building blocks" of instruction, intentionally arranged in a sequence within a grade to enable students to incrementally understand and successfully achieve a larger learning outcome. One of the great structural features of the CCSSM is that the learning progressions are not isolated and limited to any one grade level (horizontal progressions *within* a grade) but are intentionally designed as *vertical* progressions *between* grades, a carefully mapped mathematical "ascent" that begins in kindergarten and progresses upward through high school. These learning progressions have different starting and ending points. For example, whole numbers and conceptual understanding of fractions (within the Geometry domain) are the focus in grades K–2, whereas formal instruction in fractions begins in grade 3 and ends in grade 6.

With the aid of these explicit learning progressions, the authors of the CCSSM expect students to "master" the standards at one grade level by the end of each year in order to be prepared for the standards at the *next* grade level. Unlike traditional mathematics education in the United States, with each new school year beginning with an often lengthy review of math concepts and skills from prior grade levels, instruction of the CCSSM is not intended to continue this "review and repeat" approach. Instruction must build on students' *prior learning*. To meet this formidable challenge, educators will need to focus as never before on helping students attain each year's math standards as assured competencies necessary for success in the subsequent grade or course.

Jan Christinson, in his chapter "How the K–8 Learning Progressions Influence Planning for Instruction and Assessment" (2012), presents each of the math domains as a charted summary of learning progressions across several grades, accompanied by key points for educators to consider. Here, he succinctly explains how learning progressions can help students learn mathematics effectively:

> A concept is learned over time. . . . Knowledge of learning progressions can benefit the process of curriculum design, improve diagnosis of student misconceptions, inform intervention processes for students struggling in mathematics, and ultimately improve teacher knowledge of how students learn mathematics. (p. 25)

The Standards for Mathematical Practice

The Standards for Mathematical Practice describe varieties of expertise that mathematics educators at all levels should seek to develop in their students. These practices rest on important "processes and proficiencies" with longstanding importance in mathematics education [emphasized for years by the National Council of Teachers of Mathematics]: process standards of problem solving, reasoning and proof, communication, representation, and connections. [These standards also represent] the strands of mathematical proficiency specified in the National Research Council's report *Adding It Up*:

- adaptive reasoning

- strategic competence

- conceptual understanding (comprehension of mathematical concepts, operations and relations)

- procedural fluency (skill in carrying out procedures flexibly, accurately, efficiently and appropriately)

- productive disposition (habitual inclination to see mathematics as sensible, useful, and worthwhile, coupled with a belief in diligence and one's own efficacy). (CCSSI, 2010d, p. 6)

The Standards for Mathematical Practice describe ways in which students are to engage with the mathematical content throughout their elementary, middle, and high school years. These eight standards, applicable to every math domain and conceptual category, are: (1) Make sense of problems and persevere in solving them; (2) Reason abstractly and quantitatively; (3) Construct viable arguments and critique the reasoning of others; (4) Model with mathematics; (5) Use appropriate tools strategically; (6) Attend to precision; (7) Look for and make use of structure; (8) Look for and express regularity in repeated reasoning.

The Standards for Mathematical Practice are potential "points of intersection" with the Standards for Mathematical Content (CCSSI, 2010d, p.8).

Which Standards to Prioritize?

Questions often arise when groups of math educators convene to prioritize the CCSSM: "But *what* should we prioritize?—the domains, the clusters, the standards, the conceptual categories? And do we prioritize the Standards for Mathematical Practice?"

I reply by addressing the second of their questions first: "The Standards for Mathematical Practice are *not* to be prioritized. These are already priorities that are to be *continually emphasized* as students learn the Standards for Mathematical Content."

The answer to their *first* question is not as clear cut.

The Domains and Conceptual Categories

The K–8 domains and high school conceptual categories are the broad classifications, or headings, of the math standards, and all of them are also important. For example, would it be instructionally defensible in grades K–5 to prioritize Operations and Algebraic Thinking over Number and Operations in Base Ten since both of these domains include standards that all students are expected to "master" at every grade level? In high school conceptual categories, should Number and Quantity take precedence over Functions? However, contrast that line of thought with the position of the PARCC assessment consortium that asks if elementary students have "mastered knowledge and skills in highlighted domains (e.g., domain of highest importance for a particular grade level—number/fractions in grade 4; proportional reasoning and ratios in grade 6)."

Even though I present this information to math groups that gather to prioritize the CCSSM, participating educators still decide it is necessary to prioritize the standards in *each* K–8 domain. The standards within the high school conceptual categories will ultimately be assigned to high school math courses, either traditional or integrated. High school math educators are at liberty to decide whether to prioritize the course-specific standards within those courses or within the conceptual categories. Appendix A of the CCSSM provides a carefully determined assignment of the standards to traditional and integrated courses. Although it is possible to prioritize the high school math standards without referring to this document, it will save teams much time if they do.

The Clusters

The *clusters* are groups of related standards within a domain, but standards from different clusters may be grouped together. These clusters provide useful guidelines for educators as they organize and plan curriculum, instruction, and assessment.

Even though both assessment consortia agree that the CCSSM need to be prioritized, they do, however, advocate that occurring at the *cluster* level. PARCC states: "Not all of the content in a given grade is emphasized equally in the standards. *Some clusters require greater emphasis than the others* [emphasis added] based on the depth of the ideas, the time that they take [for students] to master, and/or their importance to future mathematics or to the demands of college and career readiness. In addition, an *intense focus on the most critical material at each grade* [emphasis added] allows depth in learning, which is carried out through the Standards for Mathematical Practice" (http://www.parcconline.org/parcc-model-content-frameworks/).

SBAC also recommends prioritizing the clusters and offers helpful guidance for doing so in its Appendix A: Grade-Level Content Emphases, pp. 79–86. These

provide domain-specific areas of focus for grades 3–8 and grade 11 (http://www
.smarterbalanced.org/wordpress/wp-content/uploads/2011/12/Math-Content
-Specifications.pdf).

SBAC's emphasis of certain clusters over others is an important "forecast" for
educators wanting to know which domains and related test questions will be most
represented on the new assessments. Even though educators see the value of the clusters as organizing ministructures for instruction, they do not typically prioritize the
clusters. It is helpful, however, to provide participants with the SBAC and PARCC
documents as another layer of support when choosing the Priority Standards and
throughout the vertical articulation conversations.

The Grade-Specific and Course-Specific Standards

That leaves for consideration the *grade-specific standards* within each domain in
grades K–8 and the *specific standards* (whether in traditional or integrated courses,
modified integrated courses, or from the conceptual categories) in high school. These
are the most detailed descriptions of what students need to know and be able to do,
and these are what educators prioritize.

Prioritization, Not Elimination

One of the key maxims of the Priority Standards process is "prioritization, not elimination." As stated before, those standards that will receive the *greatest emphasis* in
instruction, application, and related assessments are designated Priority Standards.
All other standards are classified as supporting standards; as their name implies,
they support, connect to, or enhance the Priority Standards. They are taught within
the context of the Priority Standards, but do not receive the same degree of instruction and assessment emphasis as do the Priority Standards. Often they provide the
instructional scaffolds needed for students to understand the more rigorous Priority Standards.

An excellent visual example of how the supporting standards can "show" how to
scaffold instruction toward the Priority Standards is represented in this grade 8 example created by San Diego Unified School District secondary math educators during professional development sessions I conducted in San Diego, California, in
October 2012 (Figure 3.2).

The document begins with the critical area of focus for a Geometry unit of study
followed by the three bolded Priority Standards for that unit. Indented supporting

<table>
<tr><td>FIGURE 3.2</td><td colspan="2">Relationship between Priority and Supporting Standards</td></tr>
</table>

Subject(s)	Mathematics—Geometry 8.G
Grade/Course	8
Unit of Study	Unit 6: "Transform Me"
Unit Type(s)	
Pacing + Buffer	20 days + 5 days

Critical Area of Focus

Students analyze two- and three-dimensional space and figures by using ideas about distance, angle, similarity, and congruence and by understanding and applying the Pythagorean theorem. They will learn the formulas for calculating the volumes of cones, cylinders, and spheres and use the formulas to solve real-world and mathematical problems. At the end of eighth grade, students will have developed a range of geometric measurement skills and an understanding of the Pythagorean theorem that will support their work in high school–level geometry.

With the aid of physical models, transparencies, and geometry software, students gain an understanding of congruence and similarity. Through experimentation, students verify the properties of rotations, reflections, and translations, including discovering that these transformations change the position of a geometric figure but not its shape or size. Students can also describe the effect of dilations (which change the size but not the shape of the figure), translations, rotations, and reflections on two-dimensional figures using coordinates on a graph. They understand that two-dimensional figures are considered *congruent* if one figure can be obtained from the other by a sequence of rotations, reflections, and translations and that the figures are considered *similar* if one figure can be obtained from the other by a sequence of dilations, rotations, reflections, and translations. Students can also describe a sequence that shows the congruence or similarity between the two figures. They use informal arguments to establish facts about the angle sum and exterior angles of triangles (e.g., consecutive exterior angles are supplementary), the angles created when parallel lines are cut by a transversal (e.g., the corresponding angles are congruent), and the angle–angle criterion for similarity of triangles (if two angles of a triangle are congruent to two angles of another triangle, the two triangles are similar).

The CCSS call for students to be formally introduced to the Pythagorean theorem in eighth grade. Under the 1997 California standards this topic is covered in seventh grade but in less depth than in the eighth-grade CCSS. Students explain a proof of the Pythagorean theorem and its converse. They apply the Pythagorean theorem to determine the side lengths in right triangles in real-world and mathematical problems in both two and three dimensions. For example, students can determine the length of the hypotenuse of a right triangle if they know the length of the two other sides. They can also use the Pythagorean theorem to find the distance between two points in a coordinate system.

(A Look at Grade 7 and 8 in California Public Schools—CDE 2012)

Continued on next page

FIGURE 3.2	**Relationship between Priority and Supporting Standards** *(continued)*

Priority Common Core State Standards **Supporting Standards**		
Understand congruence and similarity using physical models, transparencies, or geometry software.		
4.	Understand that a two-dimensional figure is similar to another if the second can be obtained from the first by a sequence of rotations, reflections, translations, and dilations; given two similar two-dimensional figures, describe a sequence that exhibits the similarity between them.	
	1.	Verify experimentally the properties of rotations, reflections, and translations: a. Lines are taken to lines, and line segments to line segments of the same length. b. Angles are taken to angles of the same measure. c. Parallel lines are taken to parallel lines.
	2.	Understand that a two-dimensional figure is congruent to another if the second can be obtained from the first by a sequence of rotations, reflections, and translations; given two congruent figures, describe a sequence that exhibits the congruence between them.
	3.	Describe the effect of dilations, translations, rotations, and reflections on two-dimensional figures using coordinates.
5.	Use informal arguments to establish facts about the angle sum and exterior angle of triangles, about the angles created when parallel lines are cut by a transversal, and the angle-angle criterion for similarity of triangles. *For example, arrange three copies of the same triangle so that the sum of the three angles appears to form a line, and give an argument in terms of transversals why this is so.*	
Understand and apply the Pythagorean Theorem.		
7.	Apply the Pythagorean Theorem to determine unknown side lengths in right triangles in real-world and mathematical problems in two and three dimensions.	
	6.	Explain a proof of the Pythagorean Theorem and its converse.
	8.	Apply the Pythagorean Theorem to find the distance between two points in a coordinate system.
Standards for Mathematical Practice **to Emphasize Throughout the Unit**		

1. Make sense of problems and persevere in solving them.
2. Reason abstractly and quantitatively.
3. Construct viable arguments and critique the reasoning of others.
4. Model with mathematics.
5. Use appropriate tools strategically.
6. Attend to precision.
7. Look for and make use of structure.
8. Look for and express regularity in repeated reasoning.

Created by Carol Achille, Taft Middle School; Dorothy D. Clater, Millennial Tech Middle; Rebecca Jimenez, Memorial Prep; Marla O'Leary, Pershing Middle. RCD – Math Cohort 1, San Diego Unified School District, October 12, 2012 standards beneath two of those three Priority Standards show the "fence post and rails" relationship. Educators will use the supporting standards (rails) as instructional scaffolds to help students acquire the more rigorous Priority Standards (fence posts). The inclusion of the eight Standards for Mathematical Practice makes explicit the connections between the SMP, the critical area of focus, and the content standards.

The prioritization process ensures that *all* standards must "figure in a mathematical education," as PARCC states in the following paragraph:

> To say that some things have greater emphasis is not to say that anything in the standards can safely be neglected in instruction. Neglecting material will leave gaps in student skill and understanding and may leave students unprepared for the challenges of a later grade. All standards figure in a mathematical education and will therefore be eligible for inclusion on the PARCC assessment and carried out through the Standards for Mathematical Practice. However, the assessments will strongly focus where the standards strongly focus. (http://www.parcconline.org/parcc-model-content-frameworks/)

Priority Standards Identification Criteria—Math

In Chapter Two, I described the process of how to prioritize the Common Core English language arts and literacy standards. All of the information in that chapter is relevant and applicable to the prioritization of the Common Core *math* standards, with one major addition to the specific criteria used to determine the priorities.

Certainly the objective criteria of endurance, leverage, and readiness for the next level of learning are important to consider in any content area, including mathematics. The authors of the CCSSM clearly recognized the importance of deep focus (prioritization) when writing the math standards and organizing them into learning progressions. To this end, they have identified *critical areas of focus* that appear in the preamble (introduction) of each grade's standards, K–8. These indicate where instructional time should focus at each of the grade levels. The critical areas of focus should factor heavily in the identification of the math Priority Standards.

Critical Areas of Focus

Focus, clarity, and specificity are key features of the Standards for Mathematical Content. The Common Core State Standards for Mathematics provides an overview of the *critical areas of focus* at each grade level that K–8 educators should reference to guide their instructional planning and emphasis throughout each school year. However, the Common Core high school standards, as written, do not provide these critical areas of focus as prominently.

Lori Cook, another of my professional development associate colleagues at The Leadership and Learning Center who specializes in the CCSSM, has noted: "There are small bits of help (regarding critical areas of focus) in Appendix A, but Massachusetts (a PARCC state) and now California (a SBAC state) are providing critical areas of focus for their high school courses, both integrated and traditional. These are great resources for high schools to reference when prioritizing the high school math standards."

In grades K–8, the content standards at each grade level specify two to four critical areas of focus for that grade, as shown in Figure 3.3.

FIGURE 3.3	**Critical Areas of Focus**

	Instructional time should focus on these critical areas:
Kindergarten	1. Representing, relating, and operating on whole numbers, initially with sets of objects.
	2. Describing shapes and space.
	More learning time in Kindergarten should be devoted to number than to other topics.
Grade 1	1. Developing understanding of addition, subtraction, and strategies for addition and subtraction within 20.
	2. Developing understanding of whole number relationships and place value, including grouping in tens and ones.
	3. Developing understanding of linear measurement and measuring lengths as iterating length units.
	4. Reasoning about attributes of, and composing and decomposing geometric shapes.
Grade 2	1. Extending understanding of base-ten notation.
	2. Building fluency with addition and subtraction.
	3. Using standard units of measure.
	4. Describing and analyzing shapes.
Grade 3	1. Developing understanding of multiplication and division and strategies for multiplication and division within 100.
	2. Developing understanding of fractions, especially unit fractions (fractions with numerator 1).
	3. Developing understanding of the structure of rectangular arrays and of area.
	4. Describing and analyzing two-dimensional shapes.
Grade 4	1. Developing understanding and fluency with multi-digit multiplication and developing understanding of dividing to find quotients involving multi-digit dividends.
	2. Developing an understanding of fraction equivalence, addition and subtraction of fractions with like denominators, and multiplication of fractions by whole numbers.
	3. Understanding that geometric figures can be analyzed and classified based on their properties, such as having parallel sides, perpendicular sides, particular angle measures, and symmetry.

FIGURE 3.3	**Critical Areas of Focus** *(continued)*

Grade 5	1. Developing fluency with addition and subtraction of fractions, and developing understanding of the multiplication of fractions and of division of fractions in limited cases (unit fractions divided by whole numbers and whole numbers divided by unit fractions).
	2. Extending division to 2-digit divisors, integrating decimal fractions into the place value system and developing understanding of operations with decimals to hundredths, and developing fluency with whole number and decimal operations.
	3. Developing understanding of volume.
Grade 6	1. Connecting ratio and rate to whole number multiplication and division and using concepts of ratio and rate to solve problems.
	2. Completing understanding of division of fractions and extending the notion of number to the system of rational numbers, which includes negative numbers.
	3. Writing, interpreting, and using expressions and equations.
	4. Developing understanding of statistical thinking.
Grade 7	1. Developing understanding of and applying proportional relationships.
	2. Developing understanding of operations with rational numbers and working with expressions and linear equations.
	3. Solving problems involving scale drawings and informal geometric constructions, and working with two- and three-dimensional shapes to solve problems involving area, surface area, and volume.
	4. Drawing inferences about population based on samples.
Grade 8	1. Formulating and reasoning about expressions and equations, including modeling an association in bivariate data with a linear equation, and solving linear equations and systems of linear equations.
	2. Grasping the concept of a function and using functions to describe quantitative relationships.
	3. Analyzing two- and three-dimensional space and figures using distance, angle, similarity, and congruence, and understanding and applying the Pythagorean Theorem.

Source: Common Core State Standards for Mathematics (CCSSI, 2010d, pp. 9, 13, 17, 21, 27, 33, 39, 46, 52).

Example: Mathematics Grade 4 Critical Areas of Focus

To illustrate with a specific grade level, shown here are the three critical areas of focus for grade 4. Each represents a different domain and is followed by its detailed summary description relative to that domain.

In Grade 4, instructional time should focus on three critical areas:

1. Developing understanding and fluency with multi-digit multiplication and developing understanding of dividing to find quotients involving multi-digit dividends;

2. Developing an understanding of fraction equivalence, addition and subtraction of fractions with like denominators, and multiplication of fractions by whole numbers; and

3. Understanding that geometric figures can be analyzed and classified based on their properties, such as having parallel sides, perpendicular sides, particular angle measures, and symmetry.

---

(1) Operations and Algebraic Thinking; Number and Operations in Base Ten. Students generalize their understanding of place value to 1,000,000, understanding the relative sizes of numbers in each place. They apply their understanding of models for multiplication (equal-sized groups, arrays, area models), place value, and properties of operations, in particular the distributive property, as they develop, discuss, and use efficient, accurate, and generalizable methods to compute products of multi-digit whole numbers. Depending on the numbers and the context, they select and accurately apply appropriate methods to estimate or mentally calculate products. They develop fluency with efficient procedures for multiplying whole numbers; understand and explain why the procedures work based on place value and properties of operations; and use them to solve problems. Students apply their understanding of models for division, place value, properties of operations, and the relationship of division to multiplication as they develop, discuss, and use efficient, accurate, and generalizable procedures to find quotients involving multi-digit dividends. They select and accurately apply appropriate methods to estimate and mentally calculate quotients, and interpret remainders based upon the context.

(2) Number and Operations—Fractions. Students develop understanding of fraction equivalence and operations with fractions. They recognize that two different fractions can be equal (e.g., 15/9 = 5/3), and they develop methods for generating and recognizing equivalent fractions. Students extend previous understandings about how fractions are built from unit fractions, composing fractions from unit fractions, decomposing fractions into unit fractions, and using the meaning of fractions and the meaning of multiplication to multiply a fraction by a whole number.

(3) Geometry. Students describe, analyze, compare, and classify two-dimensional shapes. Through building, drawing, and analyzing two-dimensional shapes, students deepen their understanding of properties of two-dimensional objects and the use of them to solve problems involving symmetry.

Using the Critical Areas of Focus to Identify the Priorities—Grade 4

When prioritizing the math standards in each of the domains, educators refer continually to this information to identify the *most comprehensive and rigorous grade-specific standards* that most closely match these critical areas of focus for the grade level. Along with the standard prioritization criteria (endurance, leverage, readiness for the next level of learning), these areas of focus should be used as the "lens" through which math educators look as they prioritize the math standards in each domain, asking themselves, "Which of these standards will most help us achieve the critical area(s) of focus for this domain?"

To illustrate, here is how the elementary educators in West Hartford, Connecticut, used the critical areas of focus to select specific standards as priorities in the domain of Operations and Algebraic Thinking in grade 4. Participants created the following chart (Figure 3.4) to show their intentional use of the critical area of focus and summary description for that domain (listed in first column) to help them select the grade 4 Priority Standards for this domain. The priorities are *bolded*, and the standards not bolded are the designated *supporting* standards.

FIGURE 3.4	Intentional Use of the Critical Area of Focus and Summary Description

	DOMAIN: Operations and Algebraic Thinking
Grade 4 Critical Area of Focus #1 and Summary Description	**Grade 4 Overview of Algebraic Thinking:** • Use the four operations with whole numbers to solve problems • Gain familiarity with factors and multiples • Generate and analyze patterns
Developing understanding and fluency with multi-digit multiplication, and developing understanding of dividing to find quotients involving multi-digit dividends. Students generalize their understanding of place value to 1,000,000, understanding the relative sizes of numbers in each place. They apply their understanding of models for multiplication (equal-sized groups, arrays, area models), place value, and properties of operations, in particular the distributive property, as they develop, discuss, and use efficient, accurate, and generalizable methods to compute products of multi-digit whole numbers. Depending on the numbers and the context, they select and accurately apply appropriate methods to estimate or mentally calculate products. They develop fluency with efficient procedures for multiplying whole numbers; understand and explain why the procedures work based on place value and properties of operations; and use them to solve problems. Students apply their understanding of models for division, place value, properties of operations, and the relationship of division to multiplication as they develop, discuss, and use efficient, accurate, and generalizable procedures to find quotients involving multi-digit dividends. They select and accurately apply appropriate methods to estimate and mentally calculate quotients, and interpret remainders based upon the context.	Priority Standards (Bolded) and Supporting Standards **4.OA.1 Interpret a multiplication equation as a comparison, e.g., interpret 35 = 5 x 7 as a statement that 35 is 5 times as many as 7 and 7 times as many as 5. Represent verbal statements of multiplicative comparisons as multiplication equations.** 4.OA.2 Multiply or divide to solve word problems involving multiplicative comparison, e.g., by using drawings and equations with a symbol for the unknown number to represent the problem, distinguishing multiplicative comparison from additive comparison. **4.OA.3 Solve multistep word problems posed with whole numbers and having whole-number answers using the four operations, including problems in which remainders must be interpreted. Represent these problems using equations with a letter standing for the unknown quantity. Assess the reasonableness of answers using mental computation and estimation strategies including rounding.** **4.OA.4 Find all factor pairs for a whole number in the range 1–100. Recognize that a whole number is a multiple of each of its factors. Determine whether a given whole number in the range 1–100 is a multiple of a given one-digit number. Determine whether a given whole number in the range 1–100 is prime or composite.** 4.OA.5 Generate a number or shape pattern that follows a given rule. Identify apparent features of the pattern that were not explicit in the rule itself. For example: Given the rule "Add 3" and the starting number 1, generate terms in the resulting sequence and observe that the terms appear to alternate between odd and even numbers. Explain informally why the numbers will continue to alternate in this way.

Example: Mathematics Grade 7 Critical Areas of Focus

As a second example, here are the four critical areas of focus for grade 7 mathematics. Each statement represents a different domain and is again followed by its detailed summary description. As with grade 4, when prioritizing the grade 7 math standards in each of the domains, educators refer continually to the grade-specific critical areas of focus to help them identify the *most comprehensive and rigorous grade-specific standards* that most closely match. Using these areas of focus as their main criteria for prioritizing, they ask themselves, "Which standards will most help us achieve the critical area(s) of focus for this domain?"

In Grade 7, instructional time should focus on four critical areas:

1. Developing understanding of and applying proportional relationships;

2. Developing understanding of operations with rational numbers and working with expressions and linear equations;

3. Solving problems involving scale drawings and informal geometric constructions, and working with two- and three-dimensional shapes to solve problems involving area, surface area, and volume; and

4. Drawing inferences about populations based on samples.

---

1. Students extend their understanding of ratios and develop understanding of proportionality to solve single- and multistep problems. Students use their understanding of ratios and proportionality to solve a wide variety of percent problems, including those involving discounts, interest, taxes, tips, and percent increase or decrease. Students solve problems about scale drawings by relating corresponding lengths between the objects or by using the fact that relationships of lengths within an object are preserved in similar objects. Students graph proportional relationships and understand the unit rate informally as a measure of the steepness of the related line, called the slope. They distinguish proportional relationships from other relationships.

2. Students develop a unified understanding of number, recognizing fractions, decimals (that have a finite or a repeating decimal representation), and percents as different representations of rational numbers. Students extend addition, subtraction, multiplication, and division to all rational numbers, maintaining the properties of operations and the relationships between addition and subtraction, and multiplication and division. By applying these properties, and by viewing negative numbers in terms of everyday contexts (e.g., amounts owed or temperatures below zero), students explain and interpret the rules for adding, subtracting, multiplying, and dividing with negative numbers. They use the arithmetic of rational numbers as they formulate expressions and equations in one variable and use these equations to solve problems.

3. Students continue their work with area from grade 6, solving problems involving the area and circumference of a circle and surface area of three-dimensional objects. In preparation for work on congruence and similarity in grade 8 they reason about relationships among two-dimensional figures using scale drawings and informal geometric constructions, and they gain familiarity with the relationships between angles formed by intersecting lines. Students work with three-dimensional figures, relating them to two-dimensional figures by examining cross-sections. They solve real-world and mathematical problems involving area, surface area, and volume of two- and three-dimensional objects composed of triangles, quadrilaterals, polygons, cubes, and right prisms.

4. Students build on their previous work with single data distributions to compare two data distributions and address questions about differences between populations. They begin informal work with random sampling to generate data sets and learn about the importance of representative samples for drawing inferences.

Using the Critical Areas of Focus to Identify the Priorities—Grade 7

The domain name Operations and Algebraic Thinking appears only in grades K–5. In the middle school grades, 6–8, that domain becomes Expressions and Equations. Here is how the middle school math team in West Hartford, Connecticut, showed the direct connections between the critical areas of focus and the standards selected (Figure 3.5). Again, the critical area of focus and summary description for that domain appear in the first column. The four priorities for the domain are *bolded*, and the two standards not bolded are the designated *supporting* standards.

FIGURE 3.5	**Direct Connections between the Critical Areas of Focus and the Standards Selected**

	DOMAIN: **Expressions and Equations**
Grade 7 **Critical Area of Focus #2 and Summary Description**	**Grade 7 Overview of Expressions and Equations:** • Use properties of operations to generate equivalent expressions. • Solve real-life and mathematical problems using numerical and algebraic expressions and equations.
Developing understanding of operations with rational numbers and working with expressions and linear equations.	Priority Standards (Bolded) and Supporting Standards
	7.EE.1 Apply properties of operations as strategies to add, subtract, factor, and expand linear expressions with rational coefficients.
Students develop a unified understanding of number, recognizing fractions, decimals (that have a finite or a repeating decimal representation), and percents as different representations of rational numbers. Students extend addition, subtraction, multiplication, and division to all rational numbers, maintaining the properties of operations and the relationships between addition and subtraction, and multiplication and division. By applying these properties, and by viewing negative numbers in terms of everyday contexts (e.g., amounts owed or temperatures below zero), students explain and interpret the rules for adding, subtracting, multiplying, and dividing with negative numbers. They use the arithmetic of rational numbers as they formulate expressions and equations in one variable and use these equations to solve problems.	7.EE.2 Understand that rewriting an expression in different forms in a problem context can shed light on the problem and how the quantities in it are related. For example, $a + 0.05a = 1.05a$ means that "increase by 5%" is the same as "multiply by 1.05."
	7.EE.3 Solve multi-step real-life and mathematical problems posed with positive and negative rational numbers in any form (whole numbers, fractions, and decimals), using tools strategically. Apply properties of operations as strategies to calculate with numbers in any form; convert between forms as appropriate; and assess the reasonableness of answers using mental computation and estimation strategies. For example: If a woman making $25 an hour gets a 10% raise, she will make an additional 1/10 of her salary an hour, or $2.50, for a new salary of $27.50. If you want to place a towel bar 9 3/4 inches long in the center of a door that is 27 1/2 inches wide, you will need to place the bar about 9 inches from each edge; this estimate can be used as a check on the exact computation.
	7.EE.4 Use variables to represent quantities in a real-world or mathematical problem, and construct simple equations and inequalities to solve problems by reasoning about the quantities. **7.EE.4a Solve word problems leading to equations of the form $px + q = r$ and $p(x + q) = r$, where p, q, and r are specific rational numbers. Solve equations of these forms fluently. Compare an algebraic solution to an arithmetic solution, identifying the sequence of the operations used in each approach. For example, the perimeter of a rectangle is 54 cm. Its length is 6 cm. What is its width?** **7.EE.4b Solve word problems leading to inequalities of the form $px + q > r$ or $px + q < r$, where p, q, and r are specific rational numbers. Graph the solution set of the inequality and interpret it in the context of the problem. For example, as a salesperson, you are paid $50 per week plus $3 per sale. This week you want your pay to be at least $100. Write an inequality for the number of sales you need to make, and describe the solutions.**

K–8 Publishers' Criteria

The Publishers' Criteria for the Common Core State Standards in Mathematics for grades K–8 state: "In high-performing countries, strong foundations are laid and then further knowledge is built on them; the design principle in those countries is *focus with coherent progressions* [emphasis added]. The U.S. has lacked such discipline" (p. 2).

Drawing on years of research and recommendations from national mathematics organizations, the authors of the Publishers' Criteria for mathematics advocate three guiding principles which can provide *another important set of criteria* to consider when prioritizing the Common Core:

Focus: Focus strongly where standards focus.

Coherence: Think across grades, and link to major topics in each grade.

Rigor: In major topics, pursue with equal intensity: conceptual understanding, procedural skill and fluency, and applications.

Here is the full text of the K–8 Publishers' Criteria as related to the criterion of "rigor." Lori Cook and I suggest sharing this text when math educators gather to prioritize the CCSSM. It will prove beneficial when trying to determine which of two standards is the more rigorous or comprehensive (i.e. the priority).

Rigor

To help students meet the expectations of the Standards, educators will need to pursue, with equal intensity, three aspects of rigor in the major work of each grade: conceptual understanding, procedural skill and fluency, and applications. The word "understand" is used in the Standards to set explicit expectations for conceptual understanding, the word "fluently" is used to set explicit expectations for fluency, and the phrase "real-world problems" and the star symbol (★) is used to set expectations and flag opportunities for applications and modeling (which is a Standard for Mathematical Practice as well as a content category in High School).

To date, curricula have not always been balanced in their approach to these three aspects of rigor. Some curricula stress fluency in computation, without acknowledging the role of conceptual understanding in attaining fluency. Some stress conceptual understanding, without acknowledging that fluency requires separate classroom work of a different nature. Some stress pure mathematics, without acknowledging first of all that applications can be highly motivating for students, and moreover, that a mathematical education should make students fit for more than just their next mathematics course. At another extreme, some curricula focus on applications, without acknowledging that math doesn't teach itself.

The Standards do not take sides in these ways, but rather they set high expectations for all three components of rigor in the major work of each grade. Of course, that makes it necessary that we first follow through on the focus in the Standards—otherwise we are asking teachers and students to do more with less.

(The Publishers' Criteria for the Common Core State Standards in Mathematics for grades K–8 are available on the Common Core Web site at http://www .corestandards.org/. Click on "Resources" on the navigation bar to access these important criteria.)

My strong recommendation to groups that gather to prioritize the math CCSS is that they have access to and study *all* of the documents and prioritization criteria showcased in this chapter with an eye to discerning the major themes, mathematical big ideas, concepts, and skills that are receiving the greatest emphasis. Almost certainly these areas of focus will translate into testable items on the SBAC and PARCC assessments. Use this information as the primary "lens" through which to look when prioritizing the math Common Core.

A Practice in Prioritizing

Before beginning the prioritization of the math standards, it is helpful to first provide participants with a "warm-up" activity. In my experience leading math groups through the process, I have found that the Geometry domain is a good starting point—first as a warm-up and then as the first domain to be prioritized—even though it is *not* emphasized as a critical area of focus for certain grade levels. However, since it is the only domain name that remains the same throughout all four grade spans, it offers an easy-to-follow, direct pathway that begins in kindergarten, continues through grade 8, and ends with high school geometry. For this warm-up, I recommend using the grade 5 Geometry domain standards. There are only four standards, two each for the two key mathematical skills. Ask participants to see which might be the "fence posts" and which the supporting "rails." Also, the Geometry domain provides participants with an easier introduction to the process of prioritizing. After learning *how* to prioritize using the Geometry standards, they are ready to repeat that process with the more challenging domains.

Prioritizing the Common Core: A Practice Activity in Mathematics

When selecting the Priority Common Core State Standards in mathematics, refer to these time-tested effective criteria for prioritizing:

- Endurance (lasting beyond one grade or course; concepts and skills needed in life)

- Leverage (crossover application within the content area and to other content areas; i.e., interdisciplinary connections)

- Readiness for the next level of learning (prerequisite concepts and skills students need to enter a new grade level or course of study)

- External Exams (state and national, college and career entrance; SBAC and PARCC information relative to prioritization).

Specific to prioritizing the Math Common Core, also keep these key points in mind:

- Understand that the CCSSM are organized according to "learning progressions"—students must learn certain concepts and skills before they are ready to learn the next ones.

- Read the critical areas of focus and summary descriptions for the entire grade level or course first.

- Then read again the critical area of focus and related summary for the domain being prioritized.

- Look for the individual standards that are the most comprehensive or rigorous, not those that are foundational.

- The Priority Standards should be the ones most likely to help students achieve the critical areas of focus.

Refer repeatedly to these critical areas of focus and summaries as the criteria for selecting the Priority Standards within each domain, grade-level, and course.

Directions for Prioritizing the Geometry Domain, Part 1

Read and discuss the critical area of focus for Grade 5 Geometry:

Students recognize volume as an attribute of three-dimensional space. They understand that volume can be measured by finding the total number of same-size units of volume required to fill the space without gaps or overlaps. They understand that a 1-unit by 1-unit by 1-unit cube is the standard unit for measuring volume. They select appropriate units, strategies, and tools for solving problems that involve estimating and measuring volume. They decompose three-dimensional shapes and find volumes of right rectangular prisms by viewing them as decomposed into layers of arrays of cubes. They measure necessary attributes of shapes in order to determine volumes to solve real-world and mathematical problems.

Directions for Prioritizing the Geometry Domain, Part 2

Referencing the critical area of focus for Grade 5 Geometry, identify two of the four Common Core State Standards as the Priority Standards—one under each bolded statement.

Common Core State Standards—Grade 5 Geometry:

Graph points on the coordinate plane to solve real-world and mathematical problems.

_____5.G.1. Use a pair of perpendicular number lines, called axes, to define a coordinate system, with the intersection of the lines (the origin) arranged to coincide with the 0 on each line and a given point in the plane located by using an ordered pair of numbers, called its coordinates. Understand that the first number indicates how far to travel from the origin in the direction of one axis, and the second number indicates how far to travel in the direction of the second axis, with the convention that the names of the two axes and the coordinates correspond (e.g., x-axis and x-coordinate, y-axis and y-coordinate).

_____5.G.2. Represent real-world and mathematical problems by graphing points in the first quadrant of the coordinate plane, and interpret coordinate values of points in the context of the situation.

Classify two-dimensional figures into categories based on their properties.

_____5.G.3. Understand that attributes belonging to a category of two-dimensional figures also belong to all subcategories of that category. For example, all rectangles have four right angles and squares are rectangles, so all squares have four right angles.

_____5.G.4. Classify two-dimensional figures in a hierarchy based on properties.

Completing the Prioritizing Steps

Following is a summary of the steps to follow when prioritizing the Common Core mathematics standards. Readers are encouraged to refer again to Chapter Two, pages 36–45, for the brief descriptions of how to complete each of the four steps for prioritizing and vertically aligning the CCSS, applicable to English language arts *and* mathematics.

- Organize by grade-span groups (K–2, 3–5, 6–8, and 9–12). If there are enough participants to form individual grade-level groups within the grade-span, each grade-level group will prioritize only the grade-level standards for their own grade.
- Select the first domain to prioritize (Geometry recommended).

  - **Step 1: Study the critical area of focus for selected domain at each grade level; Make initial selections also considering the criteria of endurance, leverage, and readiness for the next level; Reach initial consensus.**

  - **Step 2: Reference SBAC Mathematics Content Specifications or the PARCC Model Content Frameworks and the K–8 Publishers' Criteria for Mathematics (particularly the full definition of Rigor); Make changes as needed.**

  - **Step 3: Chart selections for individual grades.**

  - **Step 4: Vertically align selections K–12.**

- Resolve uncertainties; Reach large-group consensus.
- Repeat process with remaining domains.
- Prepare grade-span summaries of process followed to prioritize the CCSSM.

Achieving the Goal of the Common Core

The long-standing "coverage" approach to the teaching of state math standards will not prove effective with the Common Core State Standards for Mathematics. Prioritized CCSSM will provide educators with a sharp and consistent focus for *in-depth* instruction and related assessments and promote student attainment ("mastery," as worded in the CCSSM) of each grade's standards. The primary purpose of the Common Core State Standards Initiative is to thoroughly *prepare* all K–12 students for both college and career; these carefully selected Priority Standards will do much to help educators accomplish this goal.

READER'S ASSIGNMENT

Organize your groups of math educators and leaders to determine your own first draft of the Priority Standards for the CCSSM. Refer again to the section headings in this chapter and in Chapter Two (pages 36–45) to refresh your memory of the different tasks associated with Steps 1–4, in particular Step 4, the vertical alignment of the Priority Standards. You may also wish to refer to Chapter Eleven for a concise, step-by-step checklist to reference as you work through the process.

CHAPTER FOUR

Involving Everyone in the Process

As participants finish prioritizing and vertically aligning the K–12 Common Core standards in their respective content areas, I ask everyone, "What would happen if you returned to your schools, gave a brief explanation about the Priority Standards process to all of your colleagues who were not here during this seminar, and then shared with them these drafts? Would they be happy and ready to use them in their planning of curriculum, instruction, and assessments?"

The answer I usually receive is, "Many would, but more than likely, some would not."

"Why is that?"

"Because they wouldn't really understand what we did. They weren't involved in the process, so the resulting products wouldn't have that much meaning to them."

Whoever attends the Priority Standards work sessions—principals, assistant principals, department chairs, classroom educators, special educators, instructional specialists, curriculum coordinators, and/or central office administrators—everyone agrees that for this process to work most effectively, *the other educators* and leaders within a particular district or school need to be involved to some degree. Careful planning of how to engage all who will use the Priority Standards documents will distinguish a well-implemented idea from a poorly implemented one. In this chapter, I present effective ways in which educators can introduce both the rationale and the process for identifying the Priority Standards to those who were *not* present at the initial prioritizing sessions. But first, here is a brief overview of the final two steps of the process.

Step 5: Acquire Feedback from All

To promote a sense of "shared ownership" across the district and/or within an individual school—in both the process and the resulting products—it is recommended that feedback be acquired from all other stakeholders. Step 5 of the Priority Standards process takes place as soon as possible after seminar participants initially determine their selections. How school or district personnel successfully do this is to first explain to all who were not directly involved the rationale for prioritizing the Common Core State Standards in English language arts and mathematics. Next, they provide those colleagues with a *mini-experience* so they have the opportunity to understand the value of prioritization and how the selections were determined. Then they solicit participants' feedback on the initial drafts. This will make possible the sixth and final step in the process.

Step 6: Revise, Publish, and Distribute

The purpose of Step 6 is to incorporate the collective feedback and input from across the district or individual school(s) into a *second* draft of the Priority Standards and, if necessary, a third draft. After the final selections are decided, publish them in separate K–12 documents, one for math and the other for English language arts and literacy. These documents should contain *all* of the CCSS, with the Priority Standards bolded and the supporting standards in regular type. This will reinforce in a visual way the important message: "Prioritization, not elimination."

Creating the Priority Standards Action Plan

To plan for the accomplishment of Steps 5 and 6, create a Priority Standards Action Plan as soon as the first-draft selections have been determined, or shortly thereafter.

In a wrap-up discussion *facilitated by district and/or school administrators*, seminar participants can offer suggestions as to what their next steps should be in introducing this information to colleagues at their own schools and/or to the district as a whole. Because the participants are now thoroughly versed in both the rationale *and* the process for prioritizing the Common Core, they can offer valuable ideas about how to go about doing so.

Groups I have assisted in brainstorming this Action Plan decide to do the following:

• Create a short Priority Standards PowerPoint for administrators/lead teachers to present to staff.

• Enlist seminar participants to guide groups through the process at each school site (I recommend *partnering* of facilitators for each grade-span or content-area group so that one person is not solely responsible for this task).

• Prepare for school-site presentations by reviewing the submitted grade-span summaries of the process that was followed to prioritize the math and ELA Common Core.

• Plan a mini-experience of prioritizing either one strand of ELA (Informational Text) and/or one domain of math (Geometry) to enable colleagues to understand the process firsthand. Be sure to include the K–12 vertical alignment exercise. This will actively engage all participants and help them see how the Common Core standards connect from one grade to the next as "learning progressions."

• Discuss how to share the first-draft Priority Standards documents by content area (typically in grade-span or grade-level groups) to facilitate participant review.

• Design a feedback form for groups to fill out when reviewing the first drafts, such as the one in Figure 4.1.

• Determine dates, times, and locations for the review and feedback sessions to take place.

• Decide when to review and incorporate feedback into the next draft.

FIGURE 4.1	**Prioritizing the Common Core State Standards—Feedback Form**

Content Area: _____ Grade Level: _____ Strand or Domain: _____

Reviewed by: _____ Draft: ___ 1st ___ 2nd ___ 3rd ___ Final ___ Approved by: _____

PRIORITY Common Core State Standard (Number and Brief Description)	Endurance (lasting concepts and skills)	Leverage (applicable to other areas)	Readiness for Next Level (of schooling)	SBAC, PARCC, Publishers' Criteria for Prioritizing	K–12 Alignment Confirmed	Selection Confirmed Y/N	Notes/Comments

The Accordion Model

As described in *Power Standards* (Ainsworth, 2003a), Dr. Douglas Reeves cleverly named the orchestrated effort to involve *all* district educators and stakeholders in the prioritization decision process "The Accordion Model," using the metaphor of an accordion's outward and inward movement of its bellows. The "accordion" can be "played" in two directions—either from the district level to the school level, or vice versa.

From the District to the Schools

Curriculum coordinators prioritizing the CCSS with building representatives at a district meeting create and send first drafts of those selections to the sites (accordion out). The sites review the first drafts, provide feedback, offer suggestions for revision, and send the drafts back to the district committee (accordion in). Second drafts reflecting the feedback received are distributed again to the sites for further suggestions and/or approval (accordion out). When that feedback is returned and reviewed (accordion in), final drafts incorporating any suggested revisions are then published and distributed to all sites.

From the Schools to the District

In very large districts where it may prove difficult to assemble a cross-representation from *all* schools, administrators and educators at individual schools that participated in the initial selections of Priority Standards create and send first drafts of their documents to the district (accordion out). District administrators and content-area supervisors review the first drafts, provide feedback, offer suggestions for revision, and return the drafts to the schools (accordion in). School-level personnel consider the feedback, revise the documents, and again return them to the district supervisors (accordion out). When that feedback is reviewed and finalized (accordion in), the district publishes and distributes the Common Core Priority Standards for use at all sites.

The Accordion Model is a highly effective means for resolving differences in viewpoints. Even though it will never ensure 100 percent consensus with regard to the selections, it honors the input and feedback of *all* educators and leaders, and thus promotes a much broader acceptance of the final product district-wide.

How One District Promoted Shared Ownership

I remember how Assistant Superintendent Dr. Anne Druzolowski in West Haven, Connecticut, planned for the input and involvement of *all* educators and school leaders in finalizing the Priority Standards selections so as to ensure district-wide shared ownership.

One hundred of West Haven's 550 educators met with me in January 2009 to prioritize the *state* standards in English language arts, mathematics, science, and history/social studies. The rationale for prioritizing, the process itself, and the first-draft products were endorsed by all in attendance, but questions arose as to how the educators present would share these documents with colleagues *not* in attendance. In response to this challenge, Dr. Druzolowski scheduled several one-day Priority Standards informational sessions that I would facilitate so that everyone understood the why and how of the process.

When I subsequently met with each district group of educators over the next two months, I explained the rationale for prioritizing and then engaged those present in a mini-experience of the first four steps of the process so they could determine its value for themselves. The large K–12 group of educators at each session—now subdivided into smaller content-area groups (English language arts, math, science, and history/social studies)—made their initial selections within *one* strand, section, or domain of standards that I had preselected for them. They then discussed their selections with one another, reached initial consensus, prepared the grade-level charts, and engaged in the K–12 vertical discussion.

By the end of each of these one-day sessions, there seemed to be unanimous validation and endorsement of the Priority Standards process. I remember one educator saying enthusiastically, "Now I see what this is all about!"

I said to the whole group, "You have just experienced the process for *one* strand, domain, or section of your content-area standards. Your colleagues will be meeting with me again soon to complete first drafts of *all* the strands, domains, and sections of your content-area standards. Then they will be asking you for your feedback so any needed changes can be made before finalizing the Priority Standards for the district as a whole." Everyone appeared quite happy and satisfied with this plan. They also expressed gratitude toward their colleagues for doing this additional work for the benefit of everyone.

Why Reinvent the Wheel

Over the past decade, groups of educators within individual districts have gathered to prioritize *state* standards in virtually every content area, K–12. Neighboring districts would typically meet on their own (no collaboration across adjoining districts) to do this work. Many would question the logic of each district doing this in isolation: "Why are we reinventing the wheel and doing this work in isolation? Shouldn't we be 'working smarter and not harder' by combining our resources, personnel, and expertise to create Priority Standards that we can all share? We teach in the same state, using the same standards, so why are we going it alone?"

These questions are certainly worth asking, especially when time is so precious and budgets are so limited. Once, while I was presenting the Priority Standards information at an evening meeting attended by members of neighboring boards of education, this same issue was raised. A deputy superintendent in whose district I had conducted many professional development sessions summed up the matter in this way to the group of board members: "We questioned this at first also. But we later came to realize that our teachers had to 'have their own hands on this' for it to be widely accepted."

However, given the fact that 46 states and the District of Columbia have voluntarily adopted the CCSS, it would seem logical that more and more schools, districts, regions, and even state departments of education will now decide to partner up to prioritize and share in the creation of Common Core Priority Standards. And this may well happen even more in the coming months and years. Yet, to date, this work continues to mainly take place locally, perhaps due to the complexity of trying to coordinate scheduling of personnel in two or more districts simultaneously or simply due to past practice of working in isolation. Whether this is feasible for you to do or not, there is immense benefit in having as many of your own educators and leaders directly involved as possible. Many report that they have truly "gotten to know" the content and rigor of the Common Core as a result of their participation in the prioritization process. For that reason alone, they continue to recommend to others that they do this work themselves, even if it is happening simultaneously in a nearby district.

Prioritizing the Common Core can and will continue to take place at various organizational levels: school, district, region, and state. Steps 1–4 of the process remain the same regardless of the organizational level at which the work is done, but how Steps 5 and 6 are carried out will vary depending on that level. Here are a few suggestions to consider when determining how best to approach this work in your own setting.

Begin at the School Level

Many times this process begins randomly in a particular grade level or within an individual department of a school. Individuals return from a district or regional Priority Standards workshop and want to immediately identify the Priority Standards for the subjects they themselves teach. As more and more faculty members learn about the process, different grades or departments begin working together to determine Priority Standards for their particular content areas.

Rather than wait for this "grassroots" approach to eventually take hold in all grades and/or departments, here are ways school administrator(s) and department chairs(s) can share the Priority Standards information with everyone at the same time.

In an *elementary* building, the principal presents the rationale for prioritizing (presented in Chapter One) at a staff meeting, asks the faculty whether they would like to start with English language arts or mathematics, organizes them by grade level, and then takes them through the complete process described in Chapters Two and Three. The principal then develops with the entire faculty or grade-level representatives a timeline for completion and provides the needed support so that each grade level can meet at specific times to complete the task. When finished, the principal and faculty can repeat the entire process in the other content area. The selection of Priority Standards for the second curricular area will likely take less time than the first because everyone is now familiar with the process.

In a *secondary* building, either the principal or the assistant principal presents the information to the entire faculty, or the department chairs share the information with their colleagues at department meetings. The individual departments then decide where and when to meet as a group to determine their own content-area Priority Standards.

If the departments are large, sub-groups can be formed according to courses and grades within that discipline. For example, the math department can organize itself according to courses (algebra, geometry, algebra II, etc.), and the department members who teach those particular courses can work together to identify their related priorities. In this way, all the Priority CCSSM can be simultaneously identified in a relatively short amount of time and then compiled in a master document for reference by the entire department. But I strongly recommend that the Priority Standards selections in each course be compared/contrasted with the selections from the other math courses in order to build a "vertical map" of all the CCSSM, from one course to the next.

If the departments are small, all the educators in that department can work together to decide which course or grade to begin with, determine the Priority Standards for that course or grade, and then simply repeat the process for the remaining courses and grades. It may take longer this way since the same group of educators must do all the work, but everyone involved will have the "big picture" of which standards the group thinks are most important and how each course's Priority Standards connect to the standards in the other courses.

However educators organize themselves to work through this process, the value of the professional discussions cannot be underestimated. Not only will everyone be analyzing the Common Core in depth, but related conversations about ways to teach and assess the standards more effectively cannot help but take place.

As the faculties at individual schools hear about the Priority Standards process and begin identifying their own, sooner or later someone will ask the logical questions, "Why are we identifying our own Priority Standards when they may be different from those determined by other schools in our district? Won't this create inconsistencies rather than minimize them?"

And related questions often raised are, "Why should individual schools do the work of identifying their own Priority Standards if the goal is to eventually determine *district* Priority Standards? Why not just begin the whole process at the district level?"

Reasons for Beginning the Process at School Sites

If a district is large and not yet ready to begin this work on a district-wide scale, individual schools eager to identify their Priority Standards may not want to wait for the process to be initiated at the district level. Many times I have heard building-level administrators express their hope that the district will eventually embrace this practice, but they decide that it needs to take place right away at their own sites. They see the identification of Priority Standards as a powerful strategy for effectively understanding the standards, getting all staff "on the same page" as to what is truly important for students to know and be able to do. As more and more information continues to be released from PARCC and SBAC about the types of questions that students will encounter on the national assessments, educators are using this information to revisit and revise their initial Priority Standards selections.

Begin at the District Level

Starting with the Curriculum Coordinators

One or more curriculum coordinators from a particular school district often attend a regional Priority Standards workshop together. As they work through the activities, they discuss with each other how to *simultaneously* complete this work in their respective subject-matter areas so as to expedite the process district-wide.

The curriculum coordinators usually start by brainstorming a list of names of educators from different buildings who are experienced and highly competent in their particular content areas. They discuss inviting these individuals to a district meeting in order to recognize their expertise and ask for their assistance in the identification of Priority Standards. They decide when to schedule meetings with those individuals and plan timelines for completion of the work.

There are several benefits to beginning the Priority Standards process with the district curriculum coordinators:

1. These leaders can invite experts from a broad range of content areas from across the school system to become part of the process, ensuring representation from each school (or in the case of very large districts, areas or regions). In doing so, they are recognizing the experience and expertise of these individual educators.

2. The curriculum coordinators can share the initial information with all of these experts in the same place at the same time, ensuring that everyone hears a consistent message.

3. The curriculum coordinators can receive the valuable input from these curricular experts as they work through the Priority Standards selection process together, and then immediately schedule separate follow-up meetings for each curricular group to complete the process.

4. First drafts of the Priority Standards can thus be completed in targeted content areas in a fraction of the time it would take to finish the work in one content area before beginning it in another.

Starting with the Central Office Administrators

It takes time for a new practice or methodology, however effective it may be, to make its way through an entire school district. When central office administrators attend a Priority Standards workshop, they are thinking of the most strategic ways to implement these ideas across the district. Whether that work is begun at individual schools that will be most receptive to the practice or at district meetings attended by representatives from different buildings, central office administrators know that eventually three challenges must be addressed: (1) how to complete the prioritization of the CCSS in both English language arts and mathematics as soon as possible and practical; (2) how to involve all educators in the process for maximum effectiveness; and (3) how to then effectively *implement* the identified Priority Standards in every building in the district.

Central office administrators can accomplish the first of these three challenges by enlisting the help of their curriculum coordinators to schedule one or more district meetings—however many are needed to complete the tasks outlined in the 10-step agenda that follows—and then invite representatives from each of the buildings to be a part of the process. If any buildings have already drafted their own set of Priority CCSS in either English language arts or mathematics, the curriculum coordinators will ask those representatives to bring their drafts to the meeting.

10-Step Agenda for District Meeting(s)

The agenda for the district meeting(s) can be set as follows:

1. Establish the purpose of the meeting—identification of a common set of Priority Standards for Common Core math and/or English language arts and literacy that are representative of the combined input from educators across the district.

2. Provide the rationale and overview of the process for identifying Priority Standards in the Common Core (presented in Chapter One).

3. Divide attendees first by content areas and then ask them to sit in grade-span groups (K–2, 3–5, 6–8, and 9–12).

4. Review any drafts of identified Priority Standards brought from individual schools. Participants can either create a *second* draft of Priority Standards that reflects the combined input from those sites, or choose just to reference those documents as they create

their own first-draft Priority Standards. If no drafts are available, grade-span groups will create first-draft lists of priorities for the math domains and the ELA strands. (This is often preferred by participants, even if some do bring drafts. New groups typically want to "start fresh" and create their own selections.)

5. Complete the all-important checks for K–12 vertical alignment. Make any needed revisions.

6. Publish new or newly revised drafts for distribution and review by educators (and leaders) in all buildings.

7. Individual faculties review the district drafts of Priority Standards and offer feedback and suggestions for any needed revisions.

8. School representatives return to the *second* district Priority Standards meeting with their own faculty's feedback and proposed revisions.

9. District committee members review the feedback from sites and incorporate any agreed-upon changes into final draft revisions. (Districts may choose to ask individual sites to critique these final revisions one additional time before publication.)

10. Final drafts of the Priority Standards are published and distributed to all sites for use during the school year, with the understanding that these "final" drafts will undergo an annual review for any needed changes—at first while SBAC and PARCC continue to publish information about the 2014/15 assessments and in later years based on student performance data from those exams.

Begin at the Regional or State Level

It may be only a matter of time until regional education service agencies within states, individual state departments of education, and multiple state departments of education working collaboratively with one another come together to prioritize the CCSS. The first regional group to do this was the Northwest Regional Education Service Division (NWRESD) in Hillsboro, Oregon. In August 2011, their leaders invited me to present the Priority Standards seminar to a group of educators representing numerous school districts within their large geographical region. In Chapter

Ten, NWRESD administrators tell their story of how they successfully prioritized the CCSS in both English language arts and mathematics with representatives from numerous school disticts.

First to begin this work at the state level, the Connecticut State Department of Education asked me to present the prioritization process to a large group of invited educators from districts across the state in January 2011. After three days of professional collaboration, participants produced initial drafts of Priority Common Core Standards in both English language arts and mathematics. They then used their identified Priority Standards and related supporting standards to begin building the foundations for curricular units of study using The Leadership and Learning Center's curriculum development model, Rigorous Curriculum Design (RCD). Even though the state department of education did not formally adopt the RCD model, these initial frameworks for ELA and math units of study can be viewed online at the Connecticut state department of education Web site located at http://www.sde.ct .gov/sde/site/default.asp. Click on "Common Core State Standards in Connecticut" and then on the related links to English language arts: "K–12 ELA Units of Study," "Unit Correlations" (Priority Standards are shaded gray and supporting standards in color), and "Pacing Guides." To see the math work posted to date, click on "K–12 Math Units of Study" in its own section below English language arts. These initial unit frames are not complete; Connecticut school districts are at liberty to use these preliminary unit structures with identified Priority Standards and supporting standards as starting points for designing their own curricula.

A Preview: Six Districts Spanning East to West

To illustrate how the ideas described in this book have been successfully applied *at the district level* across the country, the next six chapters provide narrative summaries of how six different school districts in six different states identified their Priority Common Core Standards. Authored by the district leaders who directed the work, all have provided their contact information should readers wish to write or call them for further information.

There are likely to be additional questions that arise as readers consider this information and its implementation within their own particular school systems. The narratives in the following chapters will hopefully address any remaining questions you may have now, or those that may arise later when you engage in the prioritization process yourself.

READER'S ASSIGNMENT

How can you introduce the Priority Standards process in your school, district, region, or state? Develop an action plan using the following questions as guidelines to get you thinking about the most effective way to share this information and to involve all educators (and leaders) in the process. You may wish to refer again to the proposed agenda provided earlier in this chapter for district meetings to determine Priority Standards, as well as the step-by-step checklist for identifying Priority Standards in Chapter Eleven.

1. Who needs to hear this information first?

2. When and by whom will it be shared?

3. Which content area(s) should be the initial focus: English language arts, math, or both?

4. What should be your time frame for completion?

5. Which version of the Accordion Model would work best: start with schools first, then take the drafts to the district, then back to schools; OR start with the district (region, or state), send drafts to schools for feedback, and return them to the district (region, or state) for revision and publication?

CHAPTER FIVE

Greenwood School District 50, Greenwood, South Carolina

Greenwood School District 50 is a midsize district located in the western piedmont of South Carolina. The district serves approximately 9,000 students in eight elementary schools, three middle schools, and two high schools.

As the 2011/12 school year began, four words became a part of our daily vocabulary—Common Core State Standards. Early in the fall of that year, our Department of Instruction prepared to lead the transition from state standards to Common Core State Standards (CCSS). Under the guidance of Assistant Superintendent for Instruction Pat Ross, we agreed to divide grade- and subject-level groups according to our areas of expertise. ELA K–5 was assigned to Lori Cothern, ELA 6–12 was assigned to Shirley Boyce, mathematics K–5 was assigned to Dr. Pearly Milton, mathematics 6–8 was assigned to Shirley Boyce and Dr. Amy Young, and mathematics 9–12 was assigned to Dr. Amy Young. Dividing the standards in this manner made our learning curve more manageable and allowed us to focus on the structure and design of the ELA and math standards.

Faced with the implementation of the Common Core State Standards, our Department of Instruction reviewed various plans for transitioning from state standards to the CCSS. We attended workshops and conferences, participated in numerous webinars, and reviewed professional development services from numerous vendors. After hearing Steve Ventura of The Leadership and Learning Center speak at a formative assessment conference about the importance of prioritizing standards and hearing Dr. Douglas Reeves say the same during a webinar, we decided that prioritizing the standards was necessary for a successful transition to the CCSS.

In May 2012, Steve Ventura met with teams of our ELA and mathematics teachers, grades K–12. Our professional development sessions were organized into two days of mathematics focus and two days of ELA focus. Approximately 50 teachers and instructional specialists participated in each of the sessions. Three to four teachers from each grade level, grades K–5, were selected to participate in either the mathematics or ELA sessions. Teacher representatives from each grade level and each middle and high school were selected in grades 6–12.

During the professional development sessions, our teachers realized that it was okay to admit that they could not teach everything. This admission provided them with some relief and the freedom to think about the CCSS in terms of life, school, and testing. Steve led our teachers through the process of reviewing each of the standards and asking three questions:

1. What do my students need for success in *life*? (comparable to the criteria of "endurance" and "leverage")

2. What do my students need for success in *school*? (comparable to the criterion of "readiness for the next level of learning")

3. What do my students need for success on the *state test* or other high-stakes assessments? (comparable to the criterion "external exams")

The days spent with Steve were only the beginning for our teachers and our district. As the school year came to a close and throughout the summer, our lead teachers continued working with the Priority Standards to develop pacing guides and lesson plans for the 2012/13 school year and beyond.

English Language Arts

Our ELA team was composed of a minimum of three teachers from each grade level, along with at least one instructional specialist for each grade band. Included in the groups of teachers were former academic coaches and members of previous district curriculum development teams. Although we were fortunate to assemble a knowledgeable, articulate group of educators, the task of prioritizing the new CCSS was an ambitious challenge due to the minimal experience we had with this new document and the unique demands of these standards.

Prior to this initial meeting, teachers had been provided with copies of the full Common Core document, had viewed videos on the CCSS in school faculty meetings, and were provided professional resources related to the Common Core so that the team had an introductory knowledge base of the standards. As with any new task, we spent our time at the beginning of the process accessing our prior knowledge and identifying shifts in thinking that were surfacing from professional readings. The independent strengths and understandings of individuals became intertwined and resulted in rich discussions about how to approach the task of prioritizing the CCSS.

Selecting the Priority Standards—A Glimpse into Our Conversations

The ELA group began the process with the grade-level standards in the Literature strand since these standards were applicable to all grade levels of child development through grade 12. Our work began with a lengthy discussion related to the rationale and need for prioritizing the standards and the vertical articulation through all grades. At each level we puzzled through the selection of Priority Standards and often found ourselves looking at the task through a lens of curriculum development and assessment. Recognizing that standards are student learning goals, not curriculum, we felt it was valuable to reflect on current and past practice to gain clarity in selecting Priority Standards more effectively.

For example, at the elementary level our teachers had no doubt that Standards 1 and 10 met the criteria for a Priority Standard; however, after thoughtful analysis of the two, we selected Standard 1 as a Priority Standard and omitted Standard 10 from that classification. Our discussions about Standard 1 revealed that it was at the heart of moving forward with any additional standards in the Common Core document. It is the epitome of the new focus of the CCSS—close reading. Standard 10 is much more global in nature and indeed heightens teachers' attention to the new standards and demands for reading at increasing levels of text complexity. Running record assessments will be a natural measure of a student's ability to read at increasing levels of rigor. However, Standard 10 is ultimately dependent on the student's progress and understanding of the other standards outlined in the document. This initial dialogue set the tone for our remaining work and provided a productive method for discussion.

Selecting the English Language Arts Priorities—The First Two Days

During the first two days of our work, we targeted three strands of the CCSS: Literature, Informational Text, and Writing. In all three of these areas, Standards 1, 2, and 3 were quickly selected as Priority Standards. A reoccurring issue within our group was that of declassifying standards from what we called "power status." It was easy to initially select almost any standard as a life skill, and we could often justify the argument that all of the standards were essential for a productive life. So our challenge was to *not* select every standard as a priority.

A second issue that we faced in the selection of the Priority Standards was the identification of a standard as a "tested" item. Our current state multiple-choice format was the only testing background we had to draw upon. We omitted multiple standards in the selection process due to our limited knowledge of what PARCC and SBAC would emphasize as they developed test questions. A month after we finished this initial work, documents from those consortia became available that revealed a new world of testing options that we had not considered in the prioritizing phase. Though we realize this was a weakness in our initial identification of Priority Standards, we do feel that our selections of Priority CCSS will meet the current *state* testing criteria. We accepted the fact that "revision" will be a buzz word in our school system for many years to come as our depth of understanding regarding the new assessments continues to grow.

"Unwrapping" the ELA Priority Standards

The second day of this initial two-day planning session focused on "unwrapping" the English language arts Priority Standards. This process seemed to flow smoothly and actually was not as challenging as the selection of Priority Standards had been. A contributing factor to the relative ease of learning the "unwrapping" process were the discussions that we had while we identified our Priority Standards. As we prioritized, we were developing our individual and collective understanding of each standard.

Identifying the skills and concepts associated with each Priority Standard along with the level of Bloom's Taxonomy were relatively easy steps. In creating the graphic organizers to represent the "unwrapped" concepts and skills, our teachers at first referenced Bloom's Taxonomy only. However, after reviewing SBAC assessment information, we realized the need to add Webb's Depth of Knowledge (DOK) levels to our graphic organizers of the "unwrapped" standards. Karin Hess's Cognitive Rigor Matrix (http://static.pdesas.org/content/documents/M1-Slide_22_DOK_Hess _Cognitive_Rigor.pdf) provides an explanation of how to apply DOK levels to the Bloom's dimensions.

The development of the Big Idea statements and the Essential Questions harvested our greatest understanding of each standard, even though our teachers initially wrote their Big Idea statements and Essential Questions in teacher language. Our goal, as we continue to become more comfortable with the entire "unwrapping" process, is to translate our Big Ideas and Essential Questions into student-friendly language. In fact, since the initial writing of these two components, we have continued to revise our Big Ideas and Essential Questions multiple times as an integral part of our curriculum-mapping process. The team felt that when we distribute our curriculum guides to the rest of our faculty members, these Big Ideas and Essential Questions will help bring greater clarity and direction to our teachers as they begin implementation of them in their own classrooms.

Continuing the Process

After the initial two days of professional development with Steve Ventura, the grade-band teams met over the course of the next two months and reevaluated the prioritized selections for each grade level. Poster-size models of the CCSS with the Priority Standards highlighted at each grade level lined the walls in our buildings. Several hours of follow-up discussion focused on how the grade-level teams approached the task, and we looked together at the alignment of our Priority Standards across grade levels.

This period of time between the initial work and the follow-up proved advantageous. It allowed us to see our selections with a "fresh eye" and to pinpoint areas that could be unclear to teachers who had not been part of the process. Standards 1, 2, and 3 were selected at all grade levels in Literature, Informational Text, and Writing. (Author's Note: Greenwood's decision to prioritize Standards 1–3 in each of these three strands at *every* grade level—not the decision of other districts showcased in this book—highlights one of the benefits of the prioritizing process: decisions are made locally based on the collective professional judgment of the participants.) While discussing our Priority Standards we used existing print resources to confirm, refine, and clarify our understanding of key standards. After this initial conversation, grade-level groups proceeded to prioritize the standards in the remaining strands.

Kindergarten and grade 1 teachers found that their selection of Priority Standards was heavy in the area of foundational skills. At this juncture of the process, we were not confident that our decision to prioritize this area was appropriate. We based this decision on our past knowledge of curriculum, and still wonder if we need to make larger instructional shifts in this area based on Common Core expectations.

Moving from Standards to Curriculum

The second phase of the process was to use the Priority Standards to create pacing guides for the district. The focus of the group shifted from prioritizing and "unwrapping" of the standards to selecting the sequence and duration of teaching. Teachers began this curriculum development with a clearer understanding of the CCSS and a heightened sense of the instructional demands each standard would require.

We began the process of creating our pacing guides by looking at the assessment blueprint drafts published by SBAC. We collectively took sample assessments and self-scored our work based on scoring rubric guidelines. This task heightened our concern about the rigor and changes in these new standards. The exercise challenged our thinking about what we "thought we knew" and raised concerns about instructional practices and resources.

Teachers were given multiple sets of their standards that were color-coded by priority status. They took each of the Priority Standards and began to physically map out the sequence of teaching these standards across the year. Hours of conversations took place as they discussed which priority and supporting standards should be logically grouped together in the instructional sequence. Throughout the process, grade levels collaborated and shared their thoughts in order to evaluate and adjust the pacing guides.

After the initial pacing guides were decided upon, the team then began to identify resources and offer curriculum suggestions to facilitate learning in the classroom. The redesign of our curriculum was our ultimate goal as we started this entire endeavor. Without the initial steps of selecting the Priority Standards and "unwrapping" them, our curriculum development team would not have been equipped to make the important decisions necessary to produce our corresponding instructional guides.

Mathematics

The procedure for selecting members for our mathematics team was similar to the one used for the ELA team. The elementary team was composed of three to four teachers from each grade level and at least one instructional specialist for each grade band. Many of the teachers in this group had been involved in the development of our district's previous curriculum/pacing guides and were considered effective mathematics instructors.

The middle school mathematics group consisted of a teacher from each grade level (6–8) at each of the three schools along with the instructional specialist from each middle school. The high school mathematics group consisted of three teachers from each of the two schools along with the assistant principal who serves as the instructional specialist at each high school. The selection of the high school teachers was done strategically so that all math courses would be represented in the group.

Selecting the Math Priority Standards—The First Two Days

From previous professional development sessions held within our district, math teachers were familiar with the "through-line" of mathematical domains from elementary to secondary. A visual depiction of the development of domains across grade levels was shared with our teachers in February.

On the first day of our Priority Standards work session, the grades 1–5 elementary teachers began the prioritization process with the domain Number and Operations in Base Ten, followed by Number and Operations—Fractions. Kindergarten teachers began with the domain Counting and Cardinality, since this domain appears only at the kindergarten grade level. The groups then prioritized Operations and Algebraic Thinking, followed by Measurement and, last, Geometry. A grade-band matrix was created showing all of the Priority Standards selected from each domain in grades K–5 to help the team get an overall picture of which standards had been chosen. Team members reviewed this document and came to a consensus that the standards they had selected made sense.

The middle school teachers began the prioritization process with the Number System domain. From there they moved on to Expressions and Equations, Geometry, and Statistics and Probability. The teachers prioritized in this particular sequence because all of these domains were common to grades 6, 7, and 8. Then, the grade 8 teachers separately prioritized Functions (a grade 8 domain only) while the grades 6 and 7 teachers prioritized Ratios and Proportional Relationships (a domain in grades 6 and 7 only).

In South Carolina, the CCSS high school mathematics courses will be taught according to the traditional approach rather than the integrated approach. For that reason, our high school teachers referenced Appendix A of the CCSSM (www.corestandards.org/assets/CCSSI_Mathematics_Appendix_A.pdf) to determine which standards belonged to which course(s), the prioritization of the standards within those courses, and the order and pacing of the standards. Our teachers found Appendix A to be very helpful in that it took much of the guesswork out of how to organize the standards; the units and their respective standards were provided for them.

Referencing the information in Appendix A, the high school teachers took a somewhat different approach to the prioritization process. They began with a *course of study* rather than with a domain. They first prioritized the Algebra I standards. From there they moved on to Geometry and then to Algebra II. To address these two latter courses, the group subdivided into two smaller teams based on their teaching expertise. Working in this manner allowed them to prioritize all three courses and to be in a position to share their work before the school year ended with colleagues who had not been present for the prioritizing work. At this time, our high school teachers have only prioritized and paced the standards for Algebra I, Geometry, and Algebra II. We are waiting to prioritize the fourth high school math course outlined in the CCSS because we feel we need more information about what that course might be.

On the second day of professional development, the math teams learned and applied the "unwrapping" process to their newly identified Priority Common Core math standards, which also included the writing of Big Ideas and Essential Questions as described in the English language arts section of this chapter.

Continuing the Process in Math

In addition to prioritizing the Common Core mathematics standards, our teachers—elementary, middle, and high—were faced with the challenge of determining instructional gaps between the old and new standards during these transition years. This gap analysis was critical for all grades 3–11. Students in grades 3–8 will be given our state assessment test, Palmetto Assessment of State Standards (PASS), for the 2012/13 and 2013/14 school years. Students in grades 8–11 will continue to take end-of-course examinations and a high school exit exam. Some teachers who were part of the prioritization process might well agree that determining those gaps and placing related content into pacing guides with the prioritized CCSS was the most difficult part of this process. In particular, teachers of grades 3–11 know that they face the task of teaching the Common Core with a keen awareness that gaps in student knowledge will exist for several years as we transition to the CCSS.

Throughout the summer months, our teams of teachers revisited the work completed during the two-day prioritizing sessions. They visited Web sites of states that are ahead of South Carolina in the implementation process. Our teachers also devoted time to reviewing the Mathematics Content Specifications document from the Smarter Balanced Assessment Consortium Web site (www.smarterbalanced.org/smarter-balanced-assessments/). This document provides information about claims upon which all assessment questions will be based, the rationale for these claims, question formats, and sample assessment questions. We were especially interested in seeing which standards were identified as needing either major or supporting emphasis. The team compared the standards they had selected as priorities with those identified in this document to make sure no critical areas had been omitted.

The Standards for Mathematical Practice

The first Common Core professional development our teachers received was related to the Standards for Mathematical Practice (SMP). It was emphasized through Teaching Channel videos that the SMP are the *mindset* with which teachers should teach and students should learn. To keep the SMP at the forefront of all math lessons, pacing guides were designed with all eight practices listed across the bottom of each page along with a column indicating specifically which practice(s) were being addressed for that particular standard.

Sharing the Process

Comments from the group after selecting and "unwrapping" Priority Standards confirmed that this first step was vital in meeting our long-term goal of developing pacing guides and curriculum for the Common Core. Teachers in the group felt that they were leaving the sessions with a clearer understanding of the standards. Although they were aware that our work would be shared with the rest of the instructional staff of our district, they advocated for minisessions at each school to replicate the full process. Teachers viewed *the process as being of greater instructional value than the product itself,* and many said they planned to "unwrap" all standards using the strategies they had learned.

While our teachers worked to deepen their understanding of the CCSS, our principals familiarized themselves with the concept of Priority Standards and their role in implementing the CCSS. They did so by attending weekly summer leadership sessions led by members of the Department of Instruction. It was during these sessions that the district's vision for implementing the CCSS through Priority Standards was solidified. Our vision as we implement the Common Core is to increase understanding, expand abilities, and build upon previous knowledge while we prepare our students for success in college and careers.

Next Steps

During this first year of implementation of the CCSS, we will devote much time and effort to educating our parents, school board members, and community members about the Common Core. One resource we plan to use for this education process is the Parent Teacher Association (PTA) at http://www.pta.org/advocacy/content .cfm?ItemNumber=3008&navItemNumber=557.

Over the next two years, our Department of Instruction will also work to provide professional development to our teachers on Webb's Depth of Knowledge and its integration with Bloom's Taxonomy. In addition, our teachers will develop and "tweak" engaging, rigorous learning experiences and quality common assessments.

As a district, we recognize and acknowledge that we are novices in prioritizing, "unwrapping," and teaching the Common Core. We know that over the next two years we will continue to analyze our implementation practices and revise accordingly.

For more information about how Greenwood School District 50 in Greenwood, South Carolina, is implementing these professional practices, please contact:

Amy Gregory Young, Ph.D.
District Testing Coordinator—Greenwood School District 50
younga@gwd50.org
(864) 227-8845
http://www.gwd50.org/site/default.aspx?PageID=1

Leadership and Learning Center Consultant:
Steve Ventura, stephen.ventura@hmhco.com

CHAPTER SIX

Lima City School District, Lima, Ohio

The Lima City School District is a small urban district located in northwest Ohio. The district serves 4,035 students in grades K–12 and has additional services for preschoolers and adult learners. The district is made up of three small high schools within one high school building, an alternative school serving grades 5–12, one middle school serving grades 7–8, one middle school serving grades 5–6, an arts magnet school serving grades K–8, a science and technology magnet school serving grades K–8, and four traditional neighborhood elementary schools serving grades K–4.

Our student population is diverse, with 40 percent African American, 43 percent white, 14 percent multiracial, and 3 percent Hispanic. Eighty-two percent of the students within the district are identified as economically disadvantaged, and 21 percent of the population has been identified as students with disabilities. Because of the economic conditions of the community, we have a high mobility rate. Many of our students do not begin and end their school years in the district. According to the Lima City School District 2010/11 State Report Card, the district met only 5 of 26 indicators, did not meet adequate yearly progress, and did not meet the value-added measure we were aiming for, despite implementing school improvement initiatives.

Introducing the Common Core and Rigorous Curriculum Design

As the Lima City School Curriculum Office began to receive professional development on the Common Core State Standards for English language arts and mathematics as well as the Ohio Revised Standards for Social Studies and Science, there was a sense of urgency that the work begin with teachers in the district as soon as possible. In the spring of 2011 our curriculum team leaders for reading/language arts, mathematics, science, and social studies planned and provided professional development introducing the CCSS and revised state standards beginning with the K–2 grade band and high school grades 9–12. It was our intention that teachers in those grade bands would transition to the CCSS and revised state standards for the 2011/12 school year. Professional development to introduce the CCSS and revised state standards for grades 3–8 was provided throughout the 2011/12 school year.

As the curriculum team leaders observed classroom instruction in the various schools, it became clear that the K–2 transition to the CCSS was not going as well as was expected. There was some resistance among teachers who wanted to continue teaching what they had always taught and in the order they were comfortable with. Frustrated by this fact and concerned that the transition would not occur as planned, the curriculum team leaders, along with our assistant superintendent, began to research curriculum mapping and design. When we together read the book *Rigorous Curriculum Design* by Larry Ainsworth (2010), the "lightbulbs" went on. This was what we needed in our district to move our students forward!

We knew that what we were doing in our district was not resulting in the student achievement levels that we wanted, and we knew that we needed the support of experts to help move us in the right direction. None of the four curriculum team leaders had participated in curriculum design and mapping as leaders of the work, so we needed help, and we wanted to provide the best for our teachers and students. Having received in the past excellent school improvement professional development from The Leadership and Learning Center, we reached out to them again.

In organizing our district work using *Rigorous Curriculum Design*, we began with a book study for all curriculum team leaders, administrators, directors, and instructional coaches in the spring of 2012. We worked with The Leadership and Learning Center to develop a plan for professional development using the Rigorous Curriculum Design (RCD) model that would be implemented over the next two to three years in the district.

Prioritizing the CCSS—
First Foundational Step of Curriculum Redesign

The work began in the spring of 2012 with a two-day overview of RCD facilitated by Kara Vandas from The Leadership and Learning Center. We were allotted places for 30 participants, so we had to wisely select representatives from the district. The participants included building instructional coaches from each of the schools, department chairs from the high school, the curriculum team leaders, the district assistant superintendent (now superintendent), and classroom teacher representatives from each of the four targeted content areas (ELA, math, social studies, and science). District and building administrators were *not* included initially because we wanted our focus to be on those who would be doing the work in the schools throughout the process. District and building administrators were, however, updated regularly on the progress being made, and they will later be provided with professional development by those who are learning and applying the RCD process.

The two-day overview took place in mid-May of that year. Substitute teachers covered classes so that the regular teachers could attend the session. Beginning the actual work of prioritizing the Common Core took place during three consecutive days at the start of the summer break. Participants were paid to work those three extra days.

The focus of the first day was the identification of Priority Standards. Led by Kara Vandas, the participants were divided into content-specific groups. Each content-area group was facilitated by its respective district curriculum team leader. At the end of the first day, the groups had made great progress in identifying Priority Standards. By the end of the second day, all four content areas had identified their Priority Standards, completed pacing charts for grades K–12, and shared their products with the rest of the participants!

The energy in the room was unbelievable. Teachers were working together in K–12 groups for the first time, and the results were phenomenal. During the second day, many participants had already moved on to unit design using the newly identified Priority Standards, and by the end of the third day the beginnings of several units had been drafted.

Our next steps are to share the products completed during this summer work session with the rest of the district. The participants in the curriculum work (now referred to as our Curriculum Design Team) will become the leaders of this project throughout the district. These Curriculum Design Team members will be sharing with their peers an overview of the work they have completed at our district in-service day to be held during the second week of the 2012/13 school year. At that time, they will ask colleagues to review the initial drafts of Priority Standards and pacing charts and offer feedback that will be used to revise those drafts.

As the 2012/13 year begins, the Lima City Schools will ask all teachers to utilize the Priority Standards and related pacing charts. Throughout the school year, work will continue with unit design and formative assessments. Our focus for the next two years will be twofold: (1) developing and implementing rigorous curricula, and (2) forming instructional Data Teams to improve our delivery of instruction in order to increase student achievement.

Benefits of the Prioritization Process

The participants benefited from the process of prioritizing the standards in several ways. Teachers from schools across the district had the opportunity to meet, get to know each other, and work collegially on a process they were invested in. Never before have we had K–12 teachers sitting at a table together having conversations about curriculum priorities. Participants were able to take on leadership roles as a direct result of being a part of this experience. We saw an increase of buy-in by teachers regarding the need to change what we were doing in order to effectively implement the CCSS and revised state standards. As a result of their own participation in this work, the Curriculum Design Team now has a thorough understanding of the standards.

Whenever collaborative work is needed, there are inevitable challenges that arise and must be addressed. For our team, the fact that this was the first time this particular group had been expected to work together meant we had to allow time for the content teams to bond and build trust. While at times it seemed that a group might be off-task, we realized this was necessary in order for the members to get to know each other and be able to work effectively together. Accordingly, goals for the day had to be adjusted to meet group needs.

We also faced a challenge involving a few participants who believed the high school staff was already doing this work and that there was no need to redo what they were already doing. We listened to their concerns and then continued to move through the work, asking them to share what, in their eyes, had already been done. By the end of the first day of prioritizing, we overcame this challenge as participants realized that this was not just about what was happening at the high school level, but also about what was happening in the grades below. The degree of buy-in, change, and participation from some high school participants became increasingly evident as the work continued *because* we honored their initial concerns but did not allow those concerns to interfere with the work at hand.

At the beginning of our five days of professional development, some participants were apprehensive and skeptical as to why they were chosen to participate and whether the work would be beneficial. By the end of our last day, several participants indicated that this was the best professional development they had experienced in a long time. Many asked for more time together to work with teachers throughout the district and across grade levels. These validations and requests for additional opportunities to continue are among the best indicators of the success of this work.

Advice to Others

For districts considering prioritizing the CCSS in the future, our advice is to create teams of teachers that include representatives from all grade levels, K–12. In selecting participants, include those who may initially be resisters so that they participate in the work and ultimately become your advocates. This allows the challenges to be brought to the forefront of people's attention as soon as the work begins. You will then be better able to resolve these challenges before the work is rolled out to the rest of the staff.

Also, *teachers* need to be the ones prioritizing the CCSS as they are the ones who know their content areas the best and who will bear the responsibility of implementing the standards. Allow plenty of time for them to complete the work of prioritizing, so that necessary conversations can take place throughout the process. In this way, the work will not become "just another task we need to complete."

English Language Arts

As the ELA group began the work of prioritizing the CCSS, Reading Standard 10 in the Informational Text *and* Literature strands was showcased as an overarching standard for all grades. This was the only standard that the ELA group determined to be overarching for all of the ELA content. It is the goal of every grade level to have students reading and comprehending complex text at their respective grade level or grade band.

Getting started with the prioritization process seemed overwhelming at first because we were not sure where to start. Our group began with the Literature strand first because most participants felt comfortable with this section of standards. When the Literature strand was completed, the groups tackled the Informational Text standards since they seemed very similar to those in the Literature strand.

From there the group moved on to Foundational Skills (K–5). The group struggled with the K–1 Foundational Skills standards. All of them seemed to be priorities, and there was a concern that if any of them were not included in the list of Priority Standards, some teachers would not emphasize those related concepts and skills. We eventually decided to prioritize *all* of these standards in grades K–1 because they form the basis that all other standards will build upon. The group decided that fluency *through fifth grade* should be a priority because of the impact it has on comprehension, so it was included as well.

Next after the Foundational Skills, we prioritized the Writing, Speaking and Listening, and Knowledge and Use of Language strands, in that order. By the end of our first full day of work, the prioritization of all strands in all grades was completed. Day two began with the vertical alignment of the priorities to make sure that all grade levels were aligned and that there were no gaps in content and skill development.

How We Prioritized

When prioritizing the ELA Common Core State Standards, our groups began by agreeing upon the criteria that characterize a true Priority Standard. The criterion we emphasized the most was "readiness for the next level of learning." We looked for those standards that needed to be mastered in order for the student to be ready for the next grade level. Standards we identified as "fence posts" became the priorities, and the standards *supporting* those posts became "rails." While we were identifying these Priority Standards, the conversations continually circled back to assessments, and what the students would need to know and be able to do in order to be successful on those assessments.

As we looked at each grade level's Priority Standards, issues arose. It was decided ahead of time that all grade levels must align from one grade to the next. When determining vertical alignment, there had to be some "give and take" in determining which standards should be Priority Standards at certain grade levels. In some cases, Priority Standards were added to the high school list, and in others standards were removed. Because vertical alignment was essential, we knew we had to achieve consensus. The powerful benefit that came out of any disagreements that did arise was the level of the professional, collaborative conversations about curriculum and instruction that took place in order to reach agreement.

Planning District-Wide Implementation

At the conclusion of our five days of work, the team planned the "roll out" of our drafts to the rest of the ELA teachers in the district. All Priority Standards and pacing charts would be typed and then checked by the group. They would then be sent out to all teachers to review over the summer, if they chose to do so. During our fall 2012 district professional development day, each member of the group will facilitate a group review of the process and the products. These members will gather feedback on the Priority Standards and pacing charts in order that "all voices are heard" in the development of the district's CCSS Priority Standards, pacing charts, unit designs, and formative assessments. Throughout the 2012/13 school year, the pacing charts will be used by all staff and modified as needed. Units of study will be developed around the Priority Standards and shared with grade-level staff throughout the next two years. The team realizes that this is a fluid process that will continue to be developed and adapted in order to meet our students' academic needs over the coming years.

Mathematics

The mathematics group began the work of prioritizing the CCSS in mathematics with the Operations and Algebraic Thinking domain. We chose this domain because all students in all grade levels need to be able to process algebraically.

Our group identified the "through-line" domains between the elementary, middle, and high school grades based on the importance of algebra readiness as the foundation for students' success in mathematics. We carefully read and discussed the domains for each grade level. Although the mathematics domains were not titled the same for all grade levels, our group used the algebra standards as the pathway through all grade levels.

Working backward through the grades from the starting point of high school algebra, it became a challenge for our group to identify the standards needed for algebra in the lower grades. To help identify these foundational algebra standards, we asked ourselves, "How does this particular standard's concepts and skills relate to the specific algebra standards?" and then looked for examples to support our conclusions.

While prioritizing the high school math standards, we referred often to Appendix A of the Common Core math standards and the standards listed for the traditional high school math course. Referencing the clusters of math standards found in this appendix, our group was able to find and prioritize those particular standards within the clusters that would allow our students to show whether or not they had truly understood and mastered each of them; if they had, then they would certainly understand the others.

Because the high school group of teachers focused heavily on Knowledge Works, an organization working to ensure that all students in this country are prepared for college and a meaningful career (http://knowledgeworks.org/), they were comfortable looking for the standards that represented the "Big Idea." This enabled the group to prioritize the Common Core math standards up to the fourth-level math course in high school. The critical areas of focus found in the preambles for each grade in the math Common Core were also used to assist with prioritization of standards in all grade levels. The eight Standards for Mathematical Practice were continually referenced to support our decisions to make specific standards priorities.

It was very important for our group to continually remind ourselves throughout this process of the importance of algebra standards at all grade levels, starting with preschool. This was a topic we had to purposely discuss quite often.

During our fall 2012 district professional development day, our group will facilitate the review of our Priority Standards and pacing calendars. At that time, we will honor teachers' feedback regarding our work. From there, we will adjust the Priority Standards and supporting standards along with our pacing calendars for full implementation during the 2013/14 school year.

For more information about how the Lima City School District in Lima, Ohio, is implementing these powerful professional practices, please contact:

Jackie Blosser
Title I Coordinator/Curriculum Team Leader
Reading-Language Arts/District Test Coordinator
Lima City Schools

Cathy Collins
Math Curriculum Team Leader
1 Spartan Way
Lima, Ohio 45801
(419) 996-3297

Leadership and Learning Center Consultant:
Kara Vandas, kara.vandas@hmhco.com

CHAPTER SEVEN

Forsyth County Schools, Cumming, Georgia

In a suburban school district located 35 miles north of Atlanta, Georgia, administrators and teachers are embracing the adoption of Common Core State Standards and recognizing the need for focused implementation. With over 38,000 students in 36 schools, this is a large task and one that requires a systemic commitment and a process of instructional design that is clear, manageable, and yet rigorous.

Forsyth County Schools in Cumming, Georgia, has worked hard to achieve record-high levels of student performance and earn accolades at both the state and national levels. The Common Core Georgia Performance Standards were so named to help ease the transition across the state, even though they *are* the CCSS. While the adoption of these new academic standards would probably not require a great deal of increased effort on the part of our educators to maintain current levels of student performance, the district was not satisfied with that prospect. Therefore, over 18 months prior to implementation of the new standards (2012/13 in Georgia), the district engaged The Leadership and Learning Center as partners to assist us in elevating district performance to the next level. Steve Ventura, Senior Professional Development Associate with The Center, was instrumental in facilitating the work in Forsyth County Schools.

Knowledgeable about the instructional shifts required by the new Common Core English language arts and math standards, we went to work building a healthy sense of urgency between and among district and school leadership. The need was to mobilize teams and begin the work immediately in order to be prepared for these instructional shifts. Although the district had access to resources developed by the Georgia State Department of Education to help with Common Core implementation, we knew there is nothing more effective than having teachers "roll up their sleeves" and lead the work themselves. Leveraging teacher leaders always provides a better process and product, since they are the experts.

The district asked each school to form a Common Core Leadership Team, including one administrator, one ELA teacher, one math teacher, and one support teacher—ELL, gifted, or special education. These school teams of four were tapped not only to attend the professional development sessions, but also to contribute to the design of the work. The team members served as ambassadors for the Common Core in their buildings, assisting with redelivery of professional development to all staff district-wide. We began the work with an overview of the Common Core State Standards and a look at how Georgia's current standards stacked up by comparison. That same overview was provided to all staff district-wide during a professional learning day in November. Next, the teams began the process of prioritizing the standards.

Why Prioritize?

Why did Forsyth County Schools choose to prioritize the standards? The current Georgia Performance Standards (GPS) were rated by the Thomas Fordham Institute as being strongly aligned to the Common Core State Standards, which placed Georgia on solid ground for the transition (Figure 7.1). However, the hype about fewer Common Core State Standards didn't "hold up" in Forsyth County Schools. When we dug a little deeper, we noticed that while there may be fewer Common Core State Standards than Georgia Performance Standards, the complexity and performance expectations *within each standard* define a new level of rigor. This required a critical review of which standards are truly the most important. The depth and breadth of the new Common Core State Standards was the first reason we realized the need to prioritize.

Second, teachers make choices every day about the standards that they will and won't teach based on available time. This classroom-by-classroom decision making does not bode well for ensuring that the district employs a "guaranteed and viable" curriculum (Marzano, 2003). Even in the CCSS, all standards are not created equal. There are certain standards that we know should take priority over others in terms of student mastery. Therefore, the district committed to prioritizing the Common Core State Standards to alleviate the pitfalls experienced in the past that led to *covering* the content rather than *teaching* the content. The prioritization process provides teachers with a clear road map to the absolutely essential knowledge and skills students must attain.

FIGURE 7.1	How Georgia Standards Compare to the Common Core State Standards	

Thomas Fordham Institute Criteria	Georgia Performance Standards ELA	Common Core State Standards ELA
Clarity and Specificity	2/3	2/3
Content and Rigor	6/7	6/7
Total	8/10	8/10
Thomas Fordham Institute Criteria	Georgia Performance Standards Math	Common Core State Standards Math
Clarity and Specificity	3/3	2/3
Content and Rigor	6/7	7/7
Total	9/10	9/10

Let the Prioritizing Begin!

The professional development sessions were organized by grade spans, with grades K–5 and grades 6–12 attending on different days. Additionally, participants were assigned to a grade level/course (e.g., third-grade math, eighth-grade ELA). The first thing on the agenda was to provide teams with the rationale for prioritizing and a description of how the process would work. Immediately heads were nodding in agreement that not only was this needed, but also that the process would be valuable. Once presented with the three questions for determining a Priority Standard, teachers were anxious to get started, intrigued by the questions used to prioritize:

- What do students need to be successful in LIFE? (comparable to the criteria of "endurance" and "leverage")

- What do students need to be successful in SCHOOL? (comparable to the criterion of "readiness for the next level of learning")

• What do students need to be successful on the state or national TEST? (comparable to the criterion "external exams")

Forsyth County Schools' Graduate Profile

• Seek Knowledge and Understanding

• Think Critically and Solve Problems

• Listen, Communicate, and Interact Effectively

• Exhibit Strong Personal Qualities

• Use 21st-Century Learning Tools

• Engage and Compete in a Global Environment

Typically, a teacher's work is centered around what students need in order to be successful in school and on a high-stakes test. However, the teachers in Forsyth appreciated the fact that they were being asked to consider more than just content and tests. They immediately referred to the district's Graduate Profile to clarify what it means to be successful in LIFE. The Graduate Profile was developed during the district's strategic planning process in 2009 to define community commitment around what every graduate of Forsyth County Schools should know and be able to do. The six categories in the profile are more about teaching and developing the whole child rather than being just about academics. (To view the full version of our Graduate Profile, please visit our Web site at www.forsyth.k12.ga.us.) This was motivating and exciting for the teachers. In an era of accountability that tends to strangle teacher creativity, being asked the bigger question about LIFE sparked ideas about relevant, engaging learning as well.

When teachers were considering the Test criterion for prioritizing, they referenced the State Assessment Content Descriptions outlining standards assessed on the transitional state assessments (2012/13 and 2013/14 assessing the Common Core Georgia Performance Standards prior to the first statewide administration of the national assessment, PARCC, in 2014/15). Teachers were also provided the Model Content Frameworks from PARCC (www.parcconline.org/classroom) to reference when identifying Priority Standards as they relate to the new PARCC assessments. Using both of these documents helped teachers to determine the Priority Standards.

Each team was provided a copy of the Common Core State Standards not only for their assigned grade level/course, but also for the grade levels/courses above and below. The work began with the Algebra domain in math and the Reading for Informational Text strand in ELA. Referencing the agreed-upon criteria for prioritizing (essential for school, life, and the test), individuals read and marked each standard within the first strand/domain for all three grade levels/courses in the grade span with letters to indicate which criteria applied to the standard: L (LIFE), S (School), T (Test). A standard marked with all three letters would then be vetted by the entire group and considered for identification as a Priority Standard. The process requires that the individuals come to consensus and provide their colleagues with the rationale for why a particular standard should be prioritized or not. The Collaborative Decision-Making Matrix (Figure 7.2) helped to organize thoughts and ideas. The process of digging into the standards was invaluable, and teachers began to see more clearly the intentional design of the Common Core State Standards.

As soon as consensus was reached for the first strand in ELA and the first domain in math, the teams began charting their results. Each grade level/course created a large, poster-size chart listing the standard codes and a brief description of the standards. The charts were then arranged on the walls of the professional development room with all ELA prioritized standards on one side and all math prioritized stan-

FIGURE 7.2 **Collaborative Decision-Making Matrix**

Collaborative Decision-Making Matrix:
A Process to Identify Priority Standards

School/District: _____ Date: _____

Grade Level/Department: _____ Course/Content: _____

Potential Priority Standards	L Life	S School	T State/ National Test	Rigor (Bloom's or DOK)	K–12 Alignment and Feedback	Rationale for Becoming a Priority Standard

dards on the other. The participants were invited to do a "gallery walk" in teams to note the selections their colleagues had made. Within a short time the team members noted a logical learning progression across the grades. They also saw a great deal of consistency in choices from grade to grade. This step of the prioritization process helped to solidify commitment to the process, strengthen agreement that the process was indeed working, and reassure everyone that their continued efforts to prioritize *all* of the CCSS would result in a quality document to focus teaching and learning.

When prioritization and vertical alignment of the first ELA strand and the first math domain were completed, the teams went on to prioritize the other strands and domains for the grade levels/courses they were assigned. As teachers noted the shifts of certain content traditionally taught in one grade now moving to another grade in the Common Core, they became very curious about where other content had "landed" in the new standards. We noticed that teachers were moving among tables to talk to other colleagues about the content they were teaching. We realized we had created vertical teaming through the process of prioritizing! The knowledge gained by teachers related not only to their own grade-level standards, but also to the performance expectations for the grades below and above.

We also overheard teachers, who were concerned with possible new content that they would have to teach, begin to ask colleagues about pedagogy. For example, seventh-grade math teachers in Georgia are now faced with new content that was typically taught in eighth and ninth grades. They started to ask their peers who teach higher-level courses about strategies for teaching as well as ideas for instructional resources. As a district, the process of prioritizing helped us all identify areas where teachers were going to need additional content-specific professional development.

Notes about English Language Arts

Because the Common Core State Standards in English language arts are "anchored" in the College and Career Readiness Standards, the vertical alignment of strands works beautifully. There was much discussion about the importance of Reading Foundational Skills K–5 and whether or not they should all be prioritized. Our K–5 teams did prioritize only those they felt were essential and considered how reading skills should be developed grade to grade.

Reading Standard 10 was determined to be an overarching standard at every grade level/course, K–12, but was not identified as a prioritized standard. The rationale for not choosing to make Standard 10 a prioritized standard was that prioritized standards are those standards that are assessed most often. Considering that Standard 10 is intended as an end-of-the-year goal for students, *all* ELA standards at each grade level support students achieving the goal of engaging with complex text and experiencing a range of reading. Therefore, the teachers came to consensus that Standard 10 would be an Overarching Learning Goal to emphasize all year long.

Notes about Mathematics

While the Common Core offers two different pathways for mathematics, traditional and integrated, Georgia chose a path of its own. Although Integrated Mathematics was at the heart of the current Georgia Performance Standards, the decision was made to create a hybrid pathway. Courses would still be organized by standards where concepts were similar, and there would still be the expectation of including integrated performance tasks within those courses. For example, the ninth-grade course in Georgia is titled Coordinate Algebra, and the tenth-grade course is Analytic Geometry. In Forsyth we started prioritizing the Common Core for all grades 9–12 and then realized that the work would be more meaningful for teachers if they were prioritizing the standards for *each course separately,* similar to the way we were prioritizing the math standards in grades K–8. It was discussed and understood that the eight Standards for Mathematical Practice are to be emphasized *throughout* the two courses.

Forsyth's Roll-Out Plan

After prioritizing the standards, the district sought feedback on those drafts from the faculties in all of the Forsyth County schools. The prioritized standards were published online and teachers were asked for the following feedback on the standards that had and had not been listed as Priority Standards:

1. If you believe there is another standard that should be considered a Priority Standard, please provide the standard code and your rationale for inclusion.

2. If you believe there is a standard listed as a Priority Standard that should *not be,* please provide the standard code and your rationale for identification as a supporting standard.

3. Please use the space below for any questions, concerns, or feedback on the process that you may have.

The district presented the feedback received to the Common Core teams when they met to review all the feedback and make adjustments as needed. Using *Rigorous Curriculum Design* (Ainsworth, 2010) for rewriting our curricula to closely align with the Common Core, the teams continued the work by first "unwrapping" the selected Priority Standards. After that, they named the units of study for each grade and course, assigned priority and supporting standards to those units, and determined the needed pacing of those units. District curriculum design teams continued the work in the summer and developed complete Rigorous Curriculum Design units of study that included common post-assessments and engaging learning activities (authentic performance tasks).

Prioritization Is a Must

The prioritization process was a powerful kick-off to implementation of the Common Core. It allowed teachers to truly "dig into" the standards and begin to understand the performance expectations and level of rigor required of our students. As district leaders observed the groups at work, they could sense a collective sigh of relief as our teachers realized that by defining priority and supporting standards their task of designing units of study with aligned assessments would become more manageable and focused.

Prioritization is a must for any district that truly desires to provide a "guaranteed and viable curriculum" based on the new Common Core State Standards. We must give our professionals the permission to prioritize essential learning outcomes for our students. Teachers who engage in this process leave with a deeper understanding of the new standards and feel empowered to focus their instruction on what matters most. If you would like to view our district's Priority Common Core Standards, please visit our Web site at http://www.forsyth.k12.ga.us/Page/35323.

For more information about how Forsyth County Schools is implementing these professional practices, please contact:

Lissa Pijanowski, Ed.D.
Former Associate Superintendent, Academics & Accountability
Forsyth County Schools, Cumming, Georgia
770-887-2461
www.forsyth.k12.ga.us

Dr. Pijanowski is currently a Professional Development Associate
with The Leadership and Learning Center.
She can be contacted at lissa.pijanowski@hmhco.com

Leadership and Learning Center Consultant:
Steve Ventura, stephen.ventura@hmhco.com

CHAPTER EIGHT

West Hartford Public Schools, West Hartford, Connecticut

West Hartford is a city with approximately 63,000 residents located in Hartford County, Connecticut. It's a suburb of Hartford, the state's capital city. In 2010, West Hartford was named one of the nation's "10 Great Cities for Raising Families" by *Kiplinger's Personal Finance* magazine. That same year, Kiplinger's also ranked West Hartford number nine on its list of "10 Best Cities for the Next Decade."

Prekindergarten through grade 12 enrollment is slightly over 10,000 students, with eleven elementary schools, three middle schools, and two high schools. Six of the elementary schools house prekindergarten programs, and we have two elementary magnet schools.

There are 65 different languages represented in the West Hartford school system; the five largest language groups are Spanish, Mandarin, Vietnamese, Portuguese, and Russian. All 16 schools provide English as a Second Language programs, and five also provide Spanish bilingual programs.

The West Hartford public school system is a study in contrasts. The free/reduced lunch enrollment increases steadily each year, with the range of 3.5 percent eligible to 43.8 percent eligible across the 11 elementary schools. The state average for students eligible for free/reduced-price meals is 34 percent, and the average for our demographic reference group is 8.4 percent (demographic reference group: classification of districts whose students' families are similar in income, education, occupation, and need, and with roughly similar enrollment). Five of our elementary schools qualify for Title I funding.

Reasons for Prioritizing the CCSS

When the CCSS were unveiled at various state-level department venues, it became obvious to Dr. Eileen Howley, assistant superintendent, and to me that this was a "sea change" from the state standards that we had used as the basis for curriculum. While a procedure existed in West Hartford to review each curricular area on a five-year cycle, Eileen had already begun working on a *Curriculum Review and Renewal Plan for Continuous Improvement* with the goal of continuously strengthening curriculum, instruction, and assessment to enable students to be (among other things) globally competitive and "college and career ready." Our district was primed to change curriculum, and it was obvious that we needed a way to incorporate the CCSS.

After reading *Rigorous Curriculum Design* (2010) by Larry Ainsworth, Eileen and I contacted Dr. Anne Druzolowski, assistant superintendent in West Haven, Connecticut. We valued her high opinion of the work Larry had done (and was continuing to do) in her district. In September 2011, we attended The Leadership and Learning Center's Common Core Summit in New Haven, Connecticut, and realized that in order to embrace the standards and bring about a cohesive change in the way in which curriculum was written in West Hartford, we needed the Rigorous Curriculum Design (RCD) framework to help us do so.

In the past, we had prioritized state standards and "ignored those that didn't make the cut." We realized that with the CCSS, we couldn't ignore any. To set a purpose for prioritizing the Common Core, we knew we needed to frame that work within the larger context of redesigning our curricula. Toward that end, we organized an overall plan based on RCD to accomplish the project we knew would span several months.

Steps in Organizing the Work

We knew it was critical to include teachers in the Rigorous Curriculum Design process that begins with prioritizing the Common Core, but we also knew that asking teachers to be away from their students for at least nine days of professional development during the winter/spring of 2012 would prove a considerable challenge for these educators. In order to select teachers to be part of the process, we asked principals and department supervisors to consider inviting teachers who

- have exhibited leadership qualities and could successfully share this work with other colleagues;
- have exhibited expertise in their curricular area;

• have the ability to plan coherent, meaningful lessons for their students during the nine days they would be absent from the classroom;

• can commit to summer curriculum writing time; and

• understand that this would be at least a two-year commitment.

We targeted elementary ELA and math and secondary ELA, math, library media, social studies, and science for the first year of implementation. The goal for the next school year, 2012/13, would be to conduct our own internal professional development for the departments that were not included the first year.

The first group of participants included teachers, curriculum specialists (content group facilitators at the elementary level and department supervisors at the secondary level), and department supervisors. The breakdown of participants was as follows:

Elementary ELA	12
Elementary Math	12
K–12 Library Media	4
Secondary ELA	10
Secondary Math	10
Secondary Science	6
Secondary Social Studies	6

Larry facilitated our initial three-day block of professional development days in January 2012. During that time, ELA and math groups worked diligently to prioritize the Common Core. The remaining two-day blocks of professional development occurred at the end of February and again in April and May. Some groups were also able to carve out additional professional development time to continue the work in between these blocks of time.

All groups spent at least one week after school was out in June 2012 to further develop their units of study. Elementary ELA and math will have their first three units completed for implementation during the first semester of 2012/13. The math units will be ready for implementation in grades 1, 3, and 5, and the ELA units will be ready in grades K, 2, and 4. We decided to alternate grade levels at the elementary level so teachers would not have to implement new ELA *and* math units at the same time. Secondary grades are implementing units in grades 6–8 and in grades 9–10.

During the 2012/13 school year, elementary ELA and math will have mapped out the days needed to finish work on units in their current grade levels and begin work on units for the alternate grades. Secondary curriculum design groups will use their professional development time after school (regular Wednesday Curriculum and Staff Improvement) to finish the current grade-level work and move on to grades 9 and 10 curriculum development.

English Language Arts

Before we began the actual prioritizing of the Common Core ELA standards, we agreed that the criteria of "readiness for next level of learning" and "most rigorous/comprehensive versus foundational" would carry the greatest weight in making our selections. Within our *grade-level* work, teachers debated "most rigorous/comprehensive versus foundational," while in our *vertical* teams (K–12) we emphasized the "readiness for next level" factor.

We first subdivided the entire K–12 ELA content-area group into smaller grade-level and grade-span groups: K, 2, 4, 6–8, and 9–12. Within those groups we began by prioritizing the Informational Text strand, keeping in mind our agreed-upon criteria for selection. When we were finished, we came together as a K–12 vertical team to discuss, revise, and confirm our selections of Priority Standards and supporting standards. It quickly became evident that all groups had struggled with where to place Standard 10. When Larry asked if it was a Priority Standard, a supporting standard, or if it served in the role of an "overarching standard," there was a collective sigh of relief! Standard 10 actually is the umbrella under which all the other standards reside. No other standards were designated as "overarching."

Prioritization Sequence

Following the Informational Text strand, we focused on the Literature standards. After concluding our K–12 discussion about those standards (which included some healthy debate regarding certain decisions), we decided that it would be more productive for each grade-span group (K–5 and 6–12) to work on their own to prioritize the remaining strands. We all chose to begin with the Writing strand, and to follow that with Speaking and Listening.

During a week of summer 2012 curriculum writing, the K–5 Foundational Skills were prioritized (where applicable) followed by the last of the strands, Language. (As of this writing, those two areas have not yet been completed, but more summer work time is planned.) The group felt it was very important to prioritize the Foundational Skills along with the Language standards, yet to date all of these have been designated "supporting"—none have yet been identified as priority since they all support students becoming fluent readers and writers. At the elementary level, we have only completed assigning those standards to the first three units of study, and our view of whether a particular standard is priority or supporting may change as we move along.

Issues and Resolutions

We found that some supporting standards could support multiple Priority Standards. We debated whether or not a particular standard that showed up as a support under multiple priorities should be reclassified as being a priority—we decided no. At times such as these, prioritizing became somewhat difficult because we as yet do not know which concepts and skills may be heavily weighted on the Smarter Balanced assessments that Connecticut will administer for the first time in 2014/15. We decided that if we focused on the *rigor of the work* we would be fine in terms of preparation for SBAC questions.

Regarding Feedback from Those Not Involved

We have had multiple groups in the past who have prioritized state standards, and those teachers who were not directly involved readily accepted that the curriculum groups were identifying what was needed to particularly emphasize with every student. That notion prevailed with prioritization of the Common Core as well. While participants informed their peers about the work that was being done, there has not been a concern among those "back at the ranch" regarding selection of the prioritized CCSS. Faculties expressed confidence in the expertise and professional judgment of those colleagues who did the actual work of prioritizing.

Use of Prioritized Selections

Grades K, 2, and 4 teachers received their first ELA units during a professional development session on June 21, 2012. In small groups, they reviewed all aspects of the unit planner we developed. Through this review, teachers had an opportunity to become familiar with the Common Core standards and remarked that they liked the focus the Priority Standards provided.

Mathematics

We began with the thought of prioritizing the CCSS math domains through an algebra pathway. This was a complex undertaking given the volume of prerequisite knowledge necessary to build an understanding of algebra. The structure of the Common Core is such that the authors categorize the foundational learning for algebra through a numeracy pathway that builds toward an appreciation of the Real Number System, while separately identifying the more abstract algebraic thinking pathway. This pathway begins with generalizations from numerical patterning, leads into algebraic thinking, and then builds toward more complex manipulation of the algebraic constructs of expressions and equations. These two paths merge to form the body of knowledge known as algebra, which is often expressed simply as the generalization of arithmetic rules. (See Figure 8.1.)

Viewed more formally in higher mathematics, these paths merge through an understanding of fields and rings, which begins with the identification of a number

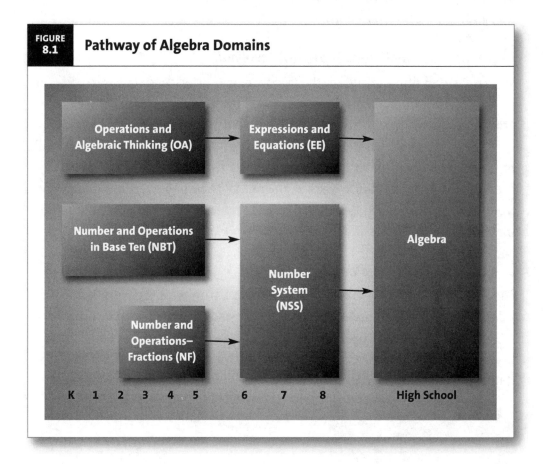

FIGURE 8.1   Pathway of Algebra Domains

system complete with at least two binary operations (call them addition and multiplication) and the requisite algebraic rules that the operations must obey (e.g., commutativity, distributivity). Seen through this lens, it is apparent that the structure of the Common Core is solidly framed around a formal approach to mathematics and develops logically through this frame.

Not surprisingly, the prioritization of standards within the algebra pathway was a long and arduous undertaking, but, I would argue, one that should be achieved with the larger picture in mind. That is to say, if one were to simply prioritize the Operations and Algebraic Thinking domain without consideration of how this domain needs to develop *in parallel with* the Number and Operations in Base Ten domain, which then leads toward the Expressions and Equations and Number Systems domains, and eventually Algebra, then the result may not necessarily reflect the greatest possible consistency of effort and foundation for the algebraic learning that is required beginning in grade 8.

Following the Mathematical "Through-Lines"

The Common Core provides guidance on how to follow a mathematical "through-line," and it is important to realize that the standards are influenced by many sources, not the least of which is the work of the National Council of Teachers of Mathematics (NCTM) and the National Research Council. In its introduction, the Common Core State Standards for Mathematics (CCSSM) reference a quote from William Schmidt and Richard Houang. They speak to the importance of paying attention not only to discrete skills but also *to the underlying concepts and conceptual framework that unify the skills* and provide a content-based context for the individual skills. Lack of this conceptual framework has long been a criticism of mathematics education in the United States. The CCSSM speak to the importance of not only giving consideration to the mathematical through-lines, but also to finding meaningful and engaging ways to

> [Content standards and curricula are coherent if they are] articulated over time as a sequence of topics and performances that are logical and reflect, where appropriate, the sequential or hierarchical nature of the disciplinary content from which the subject matter derives. That is, what and how students are taught should reflect not only the topics that fall within a certain academic discipline, but also the key ideas that determine how knowledge is organized and generated within that discipline. This implies that to be coherent, a set of content standards must evolve from particulars (e.g., the meaning and operations of whole numbers, including simple math facts and routine computational procedures associated with whole numbers and fractions) to deeper structures inherent in the discipline. These deeper structures then serve as a means for connecting the particulars (such as an understanding of the rational number system and its properties).
>
> CCSSI, 2010d, pp. 3–4

teach so as to make these through-lines apparent to students. Doing this helps students see the interconnectedness of the mathematics they are learning and understand its progression. For example, if students don't understand why we teach factoring of quadratic trinomials, then we've "missed the boat" in terms of connecting that skill to its deeper structure—whether or not the learning was sequenced *along with* the requisite emphasis within its pathway.

The through-lines that we used in West Hartford to prioritize the CCSSM borrow heavily from those identified within the NCTM Principles and Standards for School Mathematics. These principles identify a total of 10 standards (Number and Operations, Algebra, Geometry, Measurement, Data Analysis and Probability, Problem Solving, Reasoning and Proof, Communication, Connections, and Representation). The authors of the Common Core identify the intentional connections across grade-level domains in what they call "learning progressions" (see Figure 8.2). Looking at these learning progressions in conjunction with how the Common Core is organized (through domains and the eight Standards for Mathematical Practice), we

FIGURE 8.2 Connections between Common Core Math Domains

Kindergarten	1	2	3	4	5	6	7	8	HS
Counting and Cardinality									
Number and Operations in Base Ten						The Number System			Number and Quantity
			Number and Operations: Fractions			Ratios and Proportional Relationships (6 and 7)			
Operations and Algebraic Thinking						Expressions and Equations			Algebra
								Functions	Functions
Geometry						Geometry			Geometry
Measurement and Data						Statistics and Probability			Statistics and Probability

determined a set of four through-lines: Number and Quantity, Algebra, Geometry, and Statistics and Probability.

Our Choice: The Traditional Course Pathway

Our secondary mathematics program is built around the traditional course pathway of Algebra I, Geometry, and Algebra II. While we've had some discussion (both recently and in the past) about moving toward an *integrated* course approach, the Mathematics Department supervisors in West Hartford felt that the traditional approach is the appropriate direction for our district at this time.

The high school mathematics team chose to prioritize the standards independently for each course but did use Appendix A of the CCSSM as a reference to both vet and self-assess their work. This approach offered two advantages. First, it provided them with the same opportunity as the K–8 math teams to really "dig into" the standards, pour over them critically, and make their own decisions as to how they would place the standards into units of study. Second, it provided them the opportunity to consider how they would treat certain standards that clearly encompass a broad range of topics typically spanning both Algebra I and Algebra II. Given that the K–8 math standards define specific grade-level expectations and the high school math standards within conceptual categories do not, it was an important exercise for our teachers to study the standards and determine which ones could be assigned to a particular course in their entirety and which ones would need to be split over multiple courses. This same thought process also informed decisions about potential instructional approaches and learning targets (e.g., teaching linear functions alongside exponential functions with a targeted outcome of understanding the similarities and differences of those families of functions).

Prioritization Criteria

Groups prioritized the CCSSM referencing all of the following criteria, among others, to some degree: most comprehensive versus foundational, "fence post" versus "rail," critical areas of focus, and readiness for the next level of learning. Given the sequential nature of mathematics, the concepts of endurance and leverage were critical and flow naturally into that of readiness (or prerequisite) for learning at the next level. Beyond just progression of skills, more broadly defined conceptual understandings were a significant focus which forced the discussion of "fence posts" and "rails."

For example, the grade 6 Standard 6.EE.6 states: *Use variables to represent numbers and write expressions when solving a real-world or mathematical problem; under-*

stand that a variable can represent an unknown number, or, depending on the purpose at hand, any number in a specified set. This can easily be shown to be a supporting standard—"rail"—for the "fence post" standard 6.EE.7: *Solve real-world and mathematical problems by writing and solving equations of the form $x + p = q$ and $px = q$ for cases in which p, q and x are all nonnegative rational numbers.*

However, we also paid significant attention to the critical areas of focus provided by the Common Core in addition to the Grade-Level Content Emphases outlined in Appendix A of the SBAC Content Specifications. These two sources represent the authors' and the assessment consortium's opinions of what content should be prioritized or at least emphasized throughout the course of a given grade level.

In truth, our work groups struggled with prioritizing, falling victim to over-prioritizing by seldom achieving the "one-third of the total number of standards" guideline that we had used to prioritize state standards years before. I do believe that this guideline is still an important one to follow as otherwise it may send this wrong message: "If we prioritized two-thirds of the standards, what is the unspoken message about the remaining one-third?" It seems unlikely that one-third of the standards can support the remaining two-thirds, and thus the fear is that the importance of that one-third will be diminished.

This distinction between prioritizing and diminishing value was part of our groups' early conversations, but unless we were intentionally careful to abide by some guideline for prioritizing the *quantity* of standards, we may very well have fallen victim to emphasizing only certain standards and neglecting others. I plan to address the issue of the number of prioritized standards as we write and refine the curricular units of study. But in hindsight I would prefer to have held stronger to a lower number of prioritized standards from the very beginning of our prioritization work.

An Effective Process

We followed the model for prioritizing the CCSSM and then using that list of priority and supporting standards to guide placement of the math standards into units of study. The concept of Priority Standards helped with our curricular design as we were cautious to not place too many (or too few) Priority Standards within a single unit. Of equal importance was the ability to use Priority Standards to foster a vertical conversation regarding the through-lines from one grade or course to the next. This kept all grade levels focused on the progression of learning *across* grade levels instead of focusing solely on the development of learning within a single grade. Not only will the math Priority Standards guide our development of units and related assessments, they will form the basis of determining unit-based Big Ideas and Essential Questions and deciding how we frame our student learning outcomes.

Progress to Date

Our high school math team was able to prioritize the standards for Algebra I and Geometry but did not complete this task for Algebra II. Time and the size of our high school team were limiting factors that contributed to this lack of desired progress. This may prove a difficult challenge as other math teachers are included in this process. Without fully comprehending the impact of the standards on the existing Algebra II curriculum, it is possible to be short-sighted regarding the magnitude of change now necessary to make in the Algebra I curriculum. In the same way that the Common Core was developed using a backward design approach (starting with the end in mind and mapping backward from grade 12 to grade K), a true through-line cannot be established without a clear picture of the endpoint. Clearly defining the standards for Algebra II remains a priority for our high school team and should be accomplished before they move too far into the development of curricular units for Algebra I.

The Standards for Mathematical Practice

Our K–12 math group did not prioritize the eight Standards for Mathematical Practice (SMP) as we recognized the need to emphasize *all of them continually* over the course of the year. However, this is balanced with the recognition that certain units will lend themselves to more specific mathematical practices while other practices are defined more globally and will receive attention consistently *across* units of study. Within unit design, the grade-level groups are identifying which mathematical practices should naturally be emphasized to ensure that they are all attended to over time. Interestingly, in looking at the Smarter Balanced As-

Claim 1: Concepts and Procedures
Students can explain and apply mathematical concepts and interpret and carry out mathematical procedures with precision and fluency.

Claim 2: Problem Solving
Students can solve a range of complex well-posed problems in pure and applied mathematics, making productive use of knowledge and problem solving strategies.

Claim 3: Communicating Reasoning
Students can clearly and precisely construct viable arguments to support their own reasoning and to critique the reasoning of others.

Claim 4: Modeling and Data Analysis
Students can analyze complex, real-world scenarios and can construct and use mathematical models to interpret and solve problems.

sessment Consortium's proposed reporting categories, there is a de facto prioritization of the SMP.

The Content Specifications for the Summative Assessment of the Common Core State Standards for Mathematics (20 March 2012) identifies problem solving (SMP1), communicating reasoning (SMP3), and modeling and data analysis (SMP4) as *potential reporting categories* in addition to a Concepts and Procedures score (http://www.smarterbalanced.org/wordpress/wp-content/uploads/2011/12/Math-Content-Specifications.pdf).

Discussion and rationale for each reporting category are stated in terms of assessment "claims" (see text box). For example, Claim 2 states: "Students can solve a range of complex well-posed problems in pure and applied mathematics, making productive use of knowledge and problem solving strategies." In this way, SBAC folds certain mathematical practices into others in what can be construed as a supporting role. Looking for and making use of structure (SMP7) and looking for and expressing regularity in repeated reasoning (SMP8) are cited as supporting the *larger* claim related to problem solving, as is the strategic use of appropriate tools (SMP5) (SBAC, 2012).

Claim 3, "Students can clearly and precisely construct viable arguments to support their own reasoning and to critique the reasoning of others," draws a clear connection to SMP3, Construct Viable Arguments and Critique the Reasoning of Others, but is also cited as folding in SMP6, Attend to Precision.

Finally, Claim 4, "Students can analyze complex, real-world scenarios and can construct and use mathematical models to interpret and solve problems," ties directly to SMP4, Model with Mathematics, but also subsumes SMP2, Reason Abstractly and Quantitatively, and SMP5, Use Appropriate Tools Strategically.

Issues and Resolutions

One reason prioritizing the CCSSM was somewhat of an issue for our work groups was due to our history within Connecticut of prioritizing *state* standards. Given that the number of state grade-level expectations (GLEs) for which a teacher was responsible in a given grade level was too large to be a reasonable expectation for instruction, the GLEs were "prioritized" to capture assured learning experiences. Those not designated "priority" were left to be addressed as best as possible. This history placed an unfair stigma on prioritization, associating it with a practice of choosing those standards that would be taught and tested and those that likely would not.

As outlined in various sections above, the Common Core naturally "prioritizes" many of its standards, or at least *clusters* of standards, through its critical areas of focus. SBAC has done the same with its Grade-Level Content Emphases (as outlined by one of the CCSSM authors, J. Zimba; http://www.smarterbalanced.org/ wordpress/wp-content/uploads/2011/12/Math-Content-Specifications.pdf, Appendix A, pp. 79–86). Thus, there is a strong foundation within the Common Core for prioritizing. However, it is a process that must be done carefully in order to assure creation of an end product that does not differ from the original intent. In that regard, our trepidation about prioritizing was well-founded. But I do believe that this needs to be a conversation about "getting it right" rather than about whether or not to engage in the practice at all. In the end, our group did agree to follow the process of prioritizing—which led to some outstanding conversations and powerful presentations when tracing through-lines—even though some revision is necessary to improve our overall product.

Seeking Feedback; Creating a New Professional Development Model

Our secondary mathematics team decided to take on the challenge of sharing our drafts of prioritized standards and being open to receiving feedback from colleagues. During scheduled department time, the team made a presentation of their work thus far, sharing not only the product, but also the process by which it was developed. Comments from the secondary group revealed that the teachers not involved in the process said they would have benefited from even more background work with the standards before being asked to provide meaningful feedback.

Teachers at every level need the opportunity to read through and digest these standards—which is exactly what the process of prioritizing enabled our work groups to accomplish. Those outside the process need a similar opportunity in order to more fully immerse themselves in the level of change that is called for by the CCSS. While this was achieved by the secondary work group, after reflecting on their presentation to colleagues they felt there were ways they could have made the process less overwhelming for those who had been one step removed.

At the elementary level, the size of our district and our current structures did not afford an easy way to share our drafts of priority math standards with the broad audience of K–5 teachers. What we did instead was plan for a new professional development model to support not only the implementation but also the refinement of the curriculum as we implement our work during the next school year. To this end, we increased the number of content-specific professional development opportunities for K–5 teachers. We designed a structure that would provide teachers with professional development on the new units of study along with any needed background content. We planned to implement this through a district-wide grade-level setting (e.g., all third-grade teachers meeting together), while also reserving time within our professional development calendar to have small teams of grade-level teachers (3–4 schools or 10–15 teachers) conduct *horizontal* team meetings. During these meetings, teachers can engage in their own professional conversations (working with an experienced facilitator) to provide feedback on the curriculum and its implementation, and to share best practices and targeted obstacles. In this way, we hope to gain feedback on the curriculum as a whole and also on targeted issues.

Positive Benefits Both Content-Area Groups Experienced

The English language arts and math curriculum design teams all noted many positive benefits in first prioritizing the Common Core and then developing rigorous curricular units of study. Among them:

- The K–12 vertical articulation discussions provided a singular benefit. Multiple opportunities were provided for K–12 meaningful interactions. This has not been our typical way of doing curriculum work.

- Working through the process to identify Priority Standards and supporting standards helped to see where/when/why skills will be taught.

- The ability to work collaboratively was noted multiple times by all participants.

- Interdisciplinary conversations happened spontaneously yet purposefully. Science and math worked together, social studies and ELA worked together, and our Library Media specialists were tremendous assets to all!

Challenges and Resolutions

As with the introduction of any new practice into current practices, it was inevitable that certain issues would arise that we would eventually need to address. Among them were:

- Elementary math and ELA wanted to know how we would align our core math program (Trailblazers) and our core reading program (Storytown) teaching resources with our Priority Standards and new units of study.

- Secondary math questioned how we would "rearrange" the current track for students in math 6–12 and stay true to the rigorous demands of the CCSS.

- Secondary ELA pondered how to move secondary teachers away from the curriculum being "the books I love to teach" to the new units.

How did our groups resolve these and other issues? By talking, talking, and talking within grade levels, across grade levels, and across content areas. The high level of collaboration between and among our educators was amazing to watch.

Reflections and Quotes

The ultimate test for the educators who participated in the prioritization process and subsequent curriculum redesign came on June 21, 2012. June 20 was the last day of the school year for students, and June 21 was scheduled as a professional development day in which all of the new work would be introduced to teachers. First our curriculum specialists and department supervisors framed the context for the day. Then all of our curriculum design team members played a role in the presentation. They believed so strongly in the work they had done, and this came across in the marvelous way they shared with their peers what they had accomplished throughout the school year. Comments from teachers attending included:

- "Wow—the amount of superb work done to plan out the new curriculum."

- "I learned what the new objectives are as well as what things were taken away from what we currently do. I'm excited that we are all in this together, working collaboratively. I'm excited about the scope and sequence and how the units will be given to us *gradually*."

- "Learning the Essential Questions and Big Ideas will help me focus my teaching in the fall."

Our Advice to Other Groups

If we can offer any advice to other groups about how to begin the prioritization of the CCSS and the accompanying redesign of their curricula, it would be these key points:

- Make sure district and school *leaders* articulate to staff the necessity for prioritizing.

- Have as many teachers as possible do the prioritizing—don't ask administrators or a small group to do it and then "hand it down" to teachers.

- Appoint strong facilitators for each group and stay on task.

- Share across grade levels and grade spans your successes and struggles.

- Persevere through the process—it will prove to be worth it!

For more information about how West Hartford Public Schools is implementing these professional practices, please contact:

Sally Alubicki, Ed.D.
Director of Teaching and Assessment

Paul Vicinus
Director of Secondary Education
West Hartford Public Schools
50 South Main Street
West Hartford, CT 06107
860-561-6682
sally_alubicki@whps.org
paul_vicinus@whps.org

Leadership and Learning Center Consultant:
Larry Ainsworth, larry.ainsworth@hmhco.com

CHAPTER NINE

Englewood School District, Englewood, Colorado

Englewood is a small suburban community approximately 6.5 square miles in size located near the geographical center of the Denver metropolitan area. Nestled between the city of Denver and its suburbs to the south, Englewood Schools' students thrive in a unique learning environment. This public school district serves approximately 3,000 students in four elementary schools, two middle schools, two high schools, and the Early Childhood Education Center. Approximately 25 percent of all Englewood Schools' students come from outside the school district. On average, 58 percent of the students district-wide receive free or reduced-price lunches and 12 percent are homeless. Student ethnicity is predominantly either white (55 percent) or Hispanic (37 percent).

Englewood Schools has seen significant changes in the last 10 years. During that time period, eight different superintendents have led the district, which ultimately led to a scattered focus, lack of deep implementation, and a distrustful community and staff. The district school board consisted of talented, committed stakeholders who had a clear vision for the direction of the school, but with constantly changing leadership, they were unable to get a foothold into this future.

Student achievement results were in a downward trajectory for five years, with significant loss of enrollment as students fled the district looking for a more stable educational system. In 2010, Englewood was one of the bottom 11 school districts in the state of Colorado in terms of student performance, and that year posted yet another loss in terms of both achievement and student academic growth. Great things were happening in individual classrooms, but the district lacked a purposeful community and there was little common agreement on outcomes and expectations.

Our Prioritization Journey Begins

In the summer of 2010, a new era in Englewood began. With a new superintendent and a significant number of new district leaders, a commitment was made to dramatically change the future of Englewood Schools. A huge outreach effort began that included regular town hall meetings, regular shareholder reports, listening tours, focus groups, and regular meetings with the Colorado Department of Education. The district identified three specific goals that would become the "lens" through which we would look at all work for the next three years. The goals focused on improving, aligning, and reforming three keys areas of the organization: systems; postsecondary indicators; and curriculum, instruction, and assessment.

One of the first issues that needed to be addressed in the area of curriculum, instruction, and assessment was the lack of common agreement regarding instruction throughout the district. A new instructional model was created, modeled after the work of Fisher and Frey (2008), with the intentional infusion of 21st-century skills and contemporary research that supports successful teaching and learning practices.

Critical to the successful implementation of this model is the identification of Priority Standards. In the state of Colorado, the Colorado Academic Standards (CAS) serve as the expected learning targets; however, the Common Core State Standards (CCSS) are listed in their entirety *within* the Colorado documents. Because Colorado is a member of both multistate consortia—the Partnership for Assessment of Readiness for College and Careers (PARCC) *and* the Smarter Balanced Assessment Consortium (SBAC)—that are designing an assessment aligned to the CCSS, it was clear that the focus needed to be on the learning targets contained within the CCSS documents.

Gathering of Key Resources

As with any successful professional learning opportunity, as much or more time needs to go into determining expected outcomes and purposefully planning as goes into the actual strategies and activities in which teachers are engaged. Before the actual prioritization work with teachers began, various resources were gathered and utilized to prepare for that process. This allowed for some "pre" work to be done at the district level that would make the process more focused.

Because we had to work with CCSS that were already embedded by the Colorado Department of Education into the Colorado Academic Standards documents, our process for prioritizing the English language arts standards was a bit more complex than it might have been for districts in states that simply replaced all of their state standards with the Common Core.

To begin with, our district used the *Learning Progressions Frameworks Designed for Use with the Common Core State Standards in English Language Arts & Literacy K–12* by Karin K. Hess (2011). This document was cross-referenced with the CAS, and any standard that did not appear in the Learning Progressions Frameworks but *did* appear in the CAS was analyzed and ultimately removed from the document that teachers would be evaluating and prioritizing at a later time. It was decided by our Department of Curriculum that this was an acceptable "weeding" of the standards because most of the CAS were included within the CCSS, just using slightly different language. The standards that remained were then put back into the CAS format under each appropriate state standard.

All standards were double coded, once for the CAS and once for the CCSS. Englewood chose to maintain the original CAS format because unlike the CCSS, Colorado's new standards also focused on instructional resources, including Big Ideas and Essential Questions. Englewood Schools did not want teachers to lose sight of the push toward 21st-century instruction that is evident within the CAS framework. After completing this first step, our Department of Curriculum had reduced the necessary standards for each grade by a minimum of 40 percent.

Once the Department of Curriculum had this standards document that eliminated duplication between the state and national standards and also contained a prioritization that had already been completed by a highly competent national consortium, it was time to get input from the teaching staff. Because Englewood was asking teachers to analyze some of the work that had already been done at the district office and to evaluate the standards at each grade level to determine which ones should be prioritized, our Department of Curriculum was intentionally transparent about the resources that had been used to create the document. It should be noted that at any point in time the more comprehensive documents could be called upon to find standards that were deemed critical but were lost in the early prioritization efforts. These reference documents were uploaded to a wiki site and included:

- Common Core State Standards

- Colorado Academic Standards

- *Learning Progressions Frameworks Designed for Use with the Common Core State Standards in English Language Arts & Literacy K–12* (Hess, 2011).

Establishing Protocols for Work Sessions

As mentioned previously, Englewood School District was in the midst of much change at the time that the CCSS needed to be prioritized. Therefore, it was critical to rely upon input from experts in the content area of language arts at each grade level, not only to create some type of grade-level consensus, but also to allow teachers the time to collaboratively analyze the new standards and evaluate the importance of each by way of prioritization.

The work began with the end in mind, with an analysis of twelfth-grade standards. Each school sent English language arts representative teachers (generally these were teachers who were already part of the school leadership team) to a full-day prioritization session. Each session included a miniature grade-span vertical articulation team (9–12, 6–8, K–5) including same-grade teachers and teachers who taught multiple grades, therefore creating the potential for both vertical and horizontal consensus. On the first day of prioritizing there were several teachers representing grades 9–12, then on subsequent days grades 6–8 teachers came together, followed by K–5 teachers. This work continued in a similar pattern until we reached both vertical and horizontal alignment of the CCSS for grades PK–12.

Once the teachers were in the same room together, a similar protocol was followed for each work session. First teachers needed to understand how the district created the document that they would be using to analyze and prioritize standards, and then they needed to understand Colorado's commitment to joining the PARCC multistate assessment consortium (Senate Bill 12-172). Understanding this background was critical because teachers needed to refer to these primary documents when advocating for the elevation of a specific standard to priority status. Therefore, another document was uploaded to the wiki site so that teachers could refer to it at any time:

- Partnership for Assessment of Readiness for College and Careers (PARCC), Model Content Frameworks, English Language Arts/Literacy.

In addition to understanding the resources and content they would be expected to refer to during the professional learning sessions, it was imperative for teachers to understand how they would work together as a group throughout the day. Teachers were expected to use the provided resources, analyze the text, engage in critical thinking skills, and then provide evidence as to which standards were being called to the forefront based on that research. It was made clear that teachers needed to hold each other accountable for their opinions. If one teacher suggested that a specific standard should be prioritized, it was the responsibility of the group to ask for evidence as to why the standard was being considered for prioritization. Teachers would not be able to prioritize a standard because they liked it, had always taught it, or thought it was a good one. Instead their arguments needed to be supported by research found in any of the provided documents.

Teachers understood that agreement was necessary for a standard to be prioritized, and therefore a common definition for consensus was necessary. Englewood Schools chose to use the definition of consensus proposed by Rick DuFour (2010): "All points of view have been heard, and the group's will is evident, even to those who most oppose it." The purpose for clarifying how the group would work together was to make teachers comfortable with respectfully challenging each other's thinking and to support the process necessary for individuals to come to agreement.

Analyzing the Standards

After all teachers involved felt familiar enough with the available documents, resources, and boundaries for collaboration, the analysis of standards began. Because teachers needed to be able to cross-reference multiple documents that were new to them while maintaining a critical-thinking lens, a specific step-by-step analysis protocol was modeled through a think-aloud.

The think-aloud focused on only one particular standard in a strand at a central grade level. So for the 9–12 teachers, eleventh-grade Reading for All Purposes (CAS) was chosen as an exemplar. At this point, it was explained to teachers how the CAS and the CCSS were organized differently, and teachers had collaborative time to cross-reference the places where the CCSS were similar to a particular standard in the Colorado document. As soon as teachers became accustomed to flipping between different links on the wiki to align two documents that are organized very differently, step two began.

The modeling continued with the reading of the eleventh-grade portion of the PARCC Learning Progressions Frameworks that applied to the Colorado standard Reading for All Purposes. As portions of the document were read aloud, a facilitator using the numerical code in the CCSS charted any standards that were specifically named. Key skills that students were expected to be able to demonstrate as stated in the frameworks were then also added to the chart.

Once the portion of the text was completed and teachers had exhausted the list of skills and numerical standards addressed by PARCC, the facilitator demonstrated how to match phrases or numbers from the list to existing standards. If a match was found, then the facilitator highlighted that standard. Once the highlighting was complete, the teachers discussed whether they agreed that the highlighted standards should be the prioritized standards. At this point, teachers had to return to several original documents to determine one of the following:

- Should the standard be de-emphasized?
- Should the standard be reinstated (if de-emphasized by our Department of Curriculum)?
- Should the standard become a priority?

It was through this process that valuable discussion took place. In order to carry on a discussion, teachers needed to understand what the standards were asking students to know and be able to do, be able to back up their opinions with evidence, and agree upon what ultimately leads to lifelong learning. Modeling this process took about 90 minutes with teacher collaboration built in along the way. Though the process was lengthy to complete for just one strand of one grade level, it set the stage for the rest of the day's work.

When the modeling was finished, the goal was to complete one set of grade-level prioritized standards. The entire group of teachers was subdivided into three smaller groups. Each group repeated the same protocol with the next Colorado standard: Oral Expression and Listening, Writing and Composition, or Research and Reasoning. Again, the discussions about what each standard meant and whether or not a particular standard should be prioritized were the most valuable parts of the exercise.

When the small groups had prioritized the standards for their section, the whole group came back together and each small group presented their findings. At this time, members from the larger group would question, ask for clarification, or even disagree with the decisions of the smaller group. Discussion continued until whole-group consensus was reached for all standards in that grade level.

Continuing the Process

The one completed grade-level document that all 9–12 teachers in the room agreed upon was now a guide for the other grade levels. To continue, teachers were divided into groups that comprised at least one teacher at each grade level. These teachers followed the same protocol as previously explained using the PARCC documents, but had to come to agreement on a vertical articulation they thought best for students in those grade levels. These small groups addressed all four Colorado Academic Standards, and therefore all CCSS.

When the small groups came to agreement, small grade-alike groups were formed and teachers had to compare/contrast what was prioritized in each of the previous groups with their own selections. This method allowed all participants to come to the table with the interest of a student and the vertical articulation of his education as their primary focus. In the end, most of the initial groups agreed upon which standards should be prioritized at each grade level. However, this required some negotiating and some cross-table conversations in order to make final decisions. This process was repeated for each participating grade level.

Reading Standard 10

Using the CCSS, the Learning Progressions Frameworks, and the PAARC document to prioritize the standards, the participants in all grade levels noted the special attention that was drawn to particular standards. The first standard that most teachers noted was CCSS Standard 10 within literature and nonfiction: *By the end of the year, read and comprehend literary nonfiction at the high end of the grade text complexity band independently and proficiently.*

At first glance, the standard appears to be an overarching standard that is obvious in its own right and really offers no specific skill for student learning. However, upon further discussion teachers began to realize that in order for students to be able to demonstrate proficiency on any reading standard, they would need to have been practicing with text at their grade level *for the entire year*. At this point, questions about scaffolding the intensity of the reading material for less-than-proficient students came into play. Teachers came to understand that if a student needed half of the school year to become successful at comprehending and analyzing grade-level text, that same student might not have enough practice with grade-level text to perform at a proficient level on the end-of-the-year assessments.

Born of desperation and need, conversations turned to cross–content area accountability. For possibly the first time, teachers became fully aware of the purpose and importance of the interdisciplinary standards. They began to have conversations about how to help their colleagues see that reading grade-level texts in *every* class is of paramount importance for the academic growth of all students, but above all, for the less-than-proficient students. Teachers were then thrilled to find Appendix B of the CCSS, with numerous book titles included in lists of grade-level texts.

On this workday, teachers determined that the prioritization of standards should be followed by interdisciplinary conversations between teachers to build consensus on how to incorporate grade-level texts in *all* classes. Also discussed was how to scaffold instruction for student learning in ways that would allow students to read and comprehend grade-level texts as quickly as possible. In the end, it was decided by each grade level that Standard 10 in reading literature and nonfiction needed to be an *overarching standard* within the reading standards because it had a direct influence and impact on the other standards. It was too important not to be prominently emphasized throughout the Priority Standards document.

Prioritizing the Writing Strand

During the prioritization process, teachers also noted the special attention that was paid to argumentative and informative (expository) writing compared to narrative writing. Teachers were surprised to learn that even in kindergarten students were expected to write opinion pieces. As students advance through the grades, teachers found that the proportion of narrative writing decreases to only 30 percent in high school. This was a rather large shift in thinking for teachers across Englewood, as personal narrative was the primary writing genre for grades K–3, after which narrative writing accounted for about 50 percent of the expected writing curriculum in grades 4–12.

It was at this time that teachers began to discuss whether it was important to prioritize narrative writing at all. Through conversations about the stages of cognitive development and real-world writing, the decision was made to prioritize narrative writing as well as informative and opinion writing in grades K–3. In grades 4–5, narrative writing remains part of the curriculum, but it is not a prioritized focus. Finally, in grades 6–12, the genre of narrative writing has been removed from the curriculum of all language arts classes except creative writing.

As conversations about what to prioritize within the writing standards continued, teachers began to think about developing a writing rubric, or specific criteria that are expected at each grade level and within each genre of writing. Again the decision was made to follow up the prioritization workday with another session focused on revising the previous writing rubrics to match the explicit student outcomes targeted in the CCSS.

Process More Important than Product

It may be obvious that the *process* of prioritization is much more important than the completed product. Not only were teachers put in the position of analyzing and evaluating the new standards, but they also had to come to consensus regarding the final decisions. In the end, there is no end. The work has really just begun because teachers see the need to hold cross-content conversations and to align assessment rubrics/scoring guides to the expectations of the new standards. Affording teachers the time and input that is necessary for them to come to these conclusions about next steps is one of the greatest outcomes of the prioritization work.

It is interesting to note that the discussion teachers had regarding the standards found under Foundational Skills in grades K–5 focused on the fact that phonics and word recognition, and fluency and vocabulary are addressed within the Reading Literature, Reading Informational Texts, and Language standards in the Common Core. While teachers appreciated the specificity found within the K–5 Foundational Skills standards, they discussed the idea that each bulleted objective under phonics and fluency might be a skill to focus on in small, differentiated groups (depending on the needs of the group) within the bigger picture of comprehension and vocabulary.

While engaging in the work of prioritizing standards, the greatest benefit was the conversations that teachers had as a result of being given the time to analyze and evaluate the importance of each standard together in a vertical and horizontal manner. It was through discussion that teachers were not only able to come to consensus about what is most important for students to master at each grade level, but also to determine the next steps that should be completed in order for all the work to fit together into a cohesive system of improvement. To me, nothing is better than hearing teachers ask for the time to have cross-curricular conversations so that they can discuss the importance of reading grade-level texts with their grade-level colleagues or asking for more time so that they can align their assessment criteria to the expectations of the new standards. If teachers are asking for this time instead of shunning the work, progress has already been made!

Challenges, Rewards, and Consensus Building

As far as challenges go, the hardest part of the work was asking teachers to stay mentally at the second-to-highest level of Bloom's taxonomy for most of the day. The work is grueling because critical thinking at the evaluation level for long periods of time just tends to wear people out. However, the most rewarding part of the process occurred when teachers asked questions of The Leadership and Learning Center facilitator, Laura Benson. Through questions such as, "Is that right?" Laura was able to help guide the teachers in their thinking through questioning as opposed to simply providing a right answer. The best part was watching teachers having to grapple with the content and then accept themselves as being the experts.

In order to prioritize the standards, teachers needed to use the resources provided to make informed decisions. We asked them to be ready to back up their opinions with evidence about which standards should or should not be prioritized, not just rely on personal opinions or preferences. Because of their access to these resources, much of the discussion revolved around enduring understanding, readiness for the next level, and especially leverage. Leverage continued to come to the forefront because of the emphasis that the Common Core and PARCC place on grade-level reading in all content areas. Surprisingly, very few issues or disagreements arose. When one teacher did not understand why another teacher might want to elevate a particular standard to that of a prioritized standard, that teacher would simply ask, "Show where you found the importance for this standard in the research." And in the few instances when a small minority of people did not agree with the rest of the group, teachers were able to rely again on Rick DuFour's definition of consensus (2010) in order to resolve their differences of opinion.

Getting Feedback

The team began the prioritization process with the understanding that not all faculty members wanted to be involved in this work. Everyone knew they had the opportunity to either attend or send staff members who would represent them and be the voice for each grade level in each building. Once we identified those who were willing, we selected our Priority Standards through a consensus process and chose not to get feedback from staff until after another analysis of research could be conducted (which will occur after the students are assessed on only the new standards in the spring of 2015). In the meantime, the prioritized standards would be made available via the district Web site for all teachers to use to plan their instructional pacing guides and to help them identify which standards they should be using to create common formative assessments within their Data Teams.

Lessons Learned

After experiencing this process, Englewood Schools offers the following lessons learned:

- Begin with the end in mind. Start with twelfth grade and work backward to kindergarten.

- If you have to "marry" state standards with the CCSS (as we did with the Colorado Academic Standards), try to do some of the work at the district level, allowing teachers to have the ultimate say in what stays and what goes. Their input is invaluable not only because of the teachers' grade-level and content-area expertise, but because of the conversations that must take place to come to consensus.

- Have a common understanding of what consensus looks like.

- Provide resources and/or research, which teachers will be expected to use to support their opinions. Do not allow standards to be designated as Priority Standards based on opinions that have no supporting evidence.

- Allow teachers complete access to all references so that they can cross-reference any topics or ideas as necessary.

- Expect to model the type of analysis and evaluation that you want from teachers.

- Ensure time for the discussions and "back and forth" dialogue this work requires—it is the most important part of the consensus-building process and product outcomes.

- Be able to remove yourself enough from the work so that teachers experience true ownership of the final product.

For more information about how the Englewood Schools are implementing their Priority Standards for English language arts, please contact:

Dr. Karen Brofft
Assistant Superintendent, Englewood Schools
Englewood, Colorado
303-806-2003
Englewoodschools.org

Karen Brofft is currently a Professional Development Associate
with The Leadership and Learning Center.
She can be contacted at karen.brofft@hmhco.com

Leadership and Learning Center Consultant:
Laura Benson, laura.benson@hmhco.com

CHAPTER TEN

The Northwest Regional Education Service District, Hillsboro, Oregon

NWRESD is the largest education service district in the state of Oregon. It encompasses an area larger than either Delaware or Rhode Island, supports 20 school districts that have 190 schools and a student population of more than 100,000, which is approximately 20 percent of the total Oregon student population. The districts we serve range in size from 170 to 44,000 students. Our region's demographics mirror that of the state. The student population demographics are 66 percent white, 3 percent African American, 21 percent Hispanic, 5 percent Asian/Pacific Islander, 2 percent Native American, and 4 percent multiracial/ethnic.

For the past six years the districts in our region have had NWRESD focus our resources and training to support their implementation of the research-based components for improving instruction and increasing student achievement. In the fall of 2005, at the direction of our districts, NWRESD contracted with The Leadership and Learning Center to train and certify the NWRESD School Improvement Department staff in Priority Standards, "Unwrapping" Standards, Data-Driven Decision Making for Results, Data Teams, Common Formative Assessments, Effective Teaching Strategies, and Writing to Learn.

This focus has produced academic improvement within our region as measured by both grade-level and cohort results. These results are better than the state's as a whole even though the demographics, as stated, are similar. This regional data is more consistent across content areas, grades, and student sub-groups than that of other regions of the state as well. This information is important in order to provide a context for the regional discussion about the Common Core State Standards and the decision to create a regional Prioritized Common Core State Standards document.

The Decision to Prioritize
the Common Core State Standards

In the spring of 2011, the Oregon State Board of Education adopted the Common Core State Standards. The adoption of the CCSS made imperative that plans for implementation of the CCSS in each district be created at the 2011/12 meetings of the NWRESD Regional Department of Curriculum and Instruction, as well as the Regional Superintendent Council. Soon after the state board adoption, we provided districts with an analysis of the number of Common Core State Standards and

FIGURE 10.1 — **Number of Oregon Academic Content Standards by Grade Level and Content**

Grade/ Grade Level	Math	L.A.	Science	Social Studies	Sub-Total CORE	Arts	P.E.	Health	TOTAL	Instruction Hours Required
Kindergarten	15	60	9		84				84	420–420
1st	15	73	11		99				99	495–495
2nd	17	70	11		98				98	490–490
3rd	21	99	11	18	149	12	7	16	184	745–920
4th	19	108	12		139				139	695–695
5th	22	113	11	80	226	12	8	18	264	1130–1320
6th	19	113	15		147				147	735–735
7th	17	107	16		140				140	700–700
8th	20	107	17	108	252	12	13	24	301	1260–1505
9–10	40	130	32	116	318	12	14	40	384	1590–1920
11–12										

Source: Created by NWRESD School Improvement and Instruction Department.

compared them with Oregon's Academic Content Standards. It was clear to everyone that the process of prioritizing was needed as much for the CCSS as it had been for the Oregon standards. (See Figures 10.1 and 10.2 for comparison).

FIGURE 10.2	**Number of Common Core State Standards Plus Oregon Academic Content Standards**									
Grade/ Grade Level	Math	L.A.	Science	Social Studies	Sub-Total CORE	Arts	P.E.	Health	TOTAL	Instruction Hours Required
Kinder-garten	24	72	9		105				105	525-525
1st	23	82	11		116				116	580–580
2nd	27	72	11		110				110	550–550
3rd	37	91	11	18	157	12	7	16	192	785–960
4th	37	86	12		135				135	675–675
5th	40	84	11	80	215	12	8	18	253	1075–1265
6th	47	79	15 *23***	*23***	141 *187*				141 *187*	705–705 *935–935*
7th	43	76	16 *23***	*23***	135 *181*				143 *189*	675–675 *905–905*
8th	36	40	17 *23***	108 *23*	201 *247*	12	13	24	250 *296*	1005–1250 *1235–1480*
9 – 10	75*	66	32 *23***	116 *23***	289 *335*	12	14	40	355 *401*	1445–1775 *1675–2005*
11 – 12	78**	65	*22***	*22***	143 *187*				143 *187*	715–715 *935–935*

Source: Created by NWRESD School Improvement and Instruction Department and Larry Ainsworth.

Note: Numbers in **bold italic** are CCSS ELA standards required for Social Studies and Science.
 * Number of CCSS standards for grades 9–10.
** Number of CCSS standards for grades 11–12.

Figure 10.1 was created in the spring of 2006 to illustrate the number of Oregon Academic Standards. It made apparent, because of the sheer numbers, why there was a real need to prioritize them. Figure 10.2 was updated after Oregon adopted both the ELA and math Common Core State Standards in the fall of 2011.

To read the figures, find the grade level and then read horizontally to see the number of standards for each content area as well as the total number of standards and the estimated amount of instructional hours needed to teach them. Here is how these figures are organized:

1	2	3	4	5	6	7	8	9	10	11
Grade/ Grade Level	Math	L.A.	Science	Social Studies	Sub-Total CORE	Arts	P.E.	Health	TOTAL	Instruction Hours Required

- **Column 1**: Grade Level.

- **Columns 2–5 and 7–9**: Content Areas and Number of Standards in each by grade level:

  ○ Columns 2–5: CORE Content Areas that are assessed by the state or will be assessed in the future by using both the Smarter Balanced Assessment Consortium (SBAC) and Oregon State assessments.

  ○ Example: In Figure 10.2, grades 6–12, the numbers in *bold italic* are Common Core literacy standards that have been assigned to Social Studies and Science. The specific numbers are under each discipline. The *bold italic* subtotal number is the total CORE that includes both CORE and Common Core literacy standards.

- **Column 6**: Total number of CORE standards.

- **Columns 7–9**: Content Areas that are not assessed by the state or by SBAC.

- **Column 10**: Total number of standards found in all content areas.

- **Column 11**: Instructional hours required (calculated by using 5 hours for instruction, practice, feedback, and assessment multiplied by the number of standards).

  ○ Figures 10.1 and 10.2: For grades K–12, the first number is instructional hours needed for CORE standards and the second number represents hours needed for all content at that grade level.

  ○ Figure 10.2 only: For grades 6–12, bolded numbers represent instructional hours needed when adding Common Core ELA standards to each grade level's instructional responsibility.

Our analysis showed that the number of content standards had not decreased, but had increased. There were additional instructional responsibilities for secondary science and social studies teachers due to the inclusion of the 6–12 literacy standards requirements on top of their content standards. For math, not only had the number of standards increased at every grade level, but also the complexity of what was to be taught at those grade levels was greater.

In general, what was particularly noted was the complexity of the new CCSS. Discussions led teachers and administrators to see that the CCSS demands were clearer and more rigorous than those of the Oregon Academic Content Standards. In fact, one elementary teacher observed that the concepts students were asked to master and the levels of the skills that were to be demonstrated appeared one to two grade levels *earlier* in the CCSS than in the Oregon standards.

Fortunately for our region, we had entered early into the school improvement process. Prioritizing of state academic content standards had long been a focus of NWRESD districts. Identifying Priority Standards and "unwrapping" those Priority Standards provided instructional focus. The value of these processes was again recognized and the discussion quickly turned to how we could accomplish this work regionally. The same processes could later be replicated by districts as they began implementing the CCSS.

Since the state budget for districts had decreased, the rationale for a regional prioritization effort was compelling. Accomplishing the prioritization of the CCSS regionally would (1) lessen the time needed to create a starting point for district discussions and reduce the number of staff development days to do the work; (2) create a basis for similar instructional focus, thus minimizing the impact of student mobility within the region; and (3) create an atmosphere in which formative assessments could be shared across district boundaries.

Planning to Prioritize the CCSS

Using grant money provided by the Oregon Data Project, coupled with department funds, an overall plan was created. This included bringing Larry Ainsworth from The Leadership and Learning Center to lead the process. The NWRESD Department of School Improvement staff as well as staff from two other ESDs would assist Larry. Districts were invited to send elementary, middle school, and high school staff. Districts that sent representatives were: Beaverton School District, Hillsboro School District, Tigard-Tualatin School District, Gaston School District, Banks School Dis-

trict, Scappoose School District, St. Helens School District, Vernonia School District, Rainier School District, Clatskanie School District, Astoria School District,
Warrenton-Hammond School District, Jewell School District, Seaside School District, and Knappa School District. These districts represented as many as 44,000 students and as few as 170 students. A total of 70 teachers participated.

Each of the NWRESD Department of School Improvement staff members
served as a facilitator during the two days. In addition, one staff member from
Willamette ESD, one from Multnomah ESD, and a math consultant who frequently
works with NWRESD assisted in facilitation as well. All eight facilitators from the education service districts were certified in the Priority Standards process by a Leadership and Learning Center consultant who had also observed several of our
prioritizing sessions facilitated by NWRESD staff.

It should be noted that support for this regional approach was enhanced because Larry would be the lead. Larry's reputation, as well as his previous work in the
state, was admired by administrators and teachers alike across our region.

The Process

Prior to the sessions, districts provided a list of teachers with their areas of expertise.
Using this information, teachers were assigned to a content-area and grade-level
team. Both CCSS ELA and math teams had grade-span configurations of K–2, 3–5,
6–8, and 9–12. Each team had its own facilitator from the NWRESD School Improvement staff and a recorder. Larry gave specific instructions to guide the process
and served as the process "troubleshooter."

The two-day session began with Larry carefully laying out the general requirements and complexities found in the CCSS. His descriptions and examples made it
perfectly clear that without prioritizing the CCSS, teachers would be overwhelmed
by their volume and complexity. If districts didn't identify Priority Standards, individual teachers would prioritize using their own criteria and personal preferences;
the result would be a lack of K–12 content alignment and instructional focus.

A large assembly room for Larry's presentations and discussions was made available at the NWRESD facility. The work of prioritizing the CCSS ELA and math content standards was completed in separate breakout rooms, allowing grade-level teams
the needed space for their discussions and processes.

ELA and math teams used Larry's guiding principles to prioritize the CCSS. The
criteria for prioritization were: (1) What do students need for success at the *next*

level of learning? (2) Which standards represent *needed life skills (ones that would endure)?* (3) Which standards can be emphasized *across content areas (leverage)?* (4) Which standards will ensure that students do well on *standardized assessments?* Conceptually, Larry's metaphor of "fence posts and rails" was a tremendous help in focusing discussions about which standards to prioritize. In addition, he asked us to think about how many standards we should select by calculating the amount of classroom time it would take a teacher to "pre-assess, teach, assess, reteach, and reassess" each of the standards with every student.

It is important to note that the current state test, the Oregon Assessment of Knowledge and Skills (OAKS), is not aligned with the CCSS. Also, the Smarter Balanced Content Specifications had not been published at the time of this process; therefore, alignment to any standardized assessment (Step 2 of the Priority Standards process) was not completed during our initial prioritization of the Common Core.

Resources Used by the Teams

Teams were provided copies of the CCSS and their appendices to work from. In addition, copies of the NWRESD CCSS ELA and Math Navigation Tools were provided. These tools were developed to guide teachers in the transition from current state content standards to the CCSS. The Navigation Tools were created by NWRESD staff and several teachers from districts in our region to answer the following questions for teachers:

- What is similar in the Oregon Standards and the Common Core State Standards at my grade level that will still be a part of my teaching responsibility?

- What are the differences between the Oregon Standards and the Common Core State Standards at my grade level that I will now be responsible to teach?

- What language changes have been made with respect to rigor in skills?

- What do I no longer teach, and who will be teaching it instead?

The process of creating the document allowed us, as School Improvement Specialists, to look at the CCSS in depth and be confident in our understanding of the standards. The tools have been used by numerous educators throughout Oregon as a vehicle for understanding the impact of the CCSS on both teachers and students. The Navigation Tools can be found at http://et.nwresd.org under Common Core State Standards.

Prioritizing the Math CCSS

As the math teams looked at the CCSS, it was decided to first review the NWRESD CCSS Navigation Tool, and then teams would align the domains visually onto chart-sized posters to facilitate discussions. Following are the two charts that were created (Figures 10.3 and 10.4). Figure 10.3 shows the CCSS math domains as presented in the documents. Figure 10.4 shows the CCSS domains aligned across grade levels (this chart was created at the start of the regional process).

| FIGURE 10.3 | **Common Core State Standards—Math Domain Organization** |

K–2	3–5	6–7	8	High School
Counting and Cardinality (K only)	Operations and Algebraic Thinking	Ratio and Proportion	Number System	Number and Quantity
Operations and Algebraic Thinking	Number and Operations in Base Ten	The Number System	Expressions and Equations	Algebra
Number and Operations in Base Ten	Number and Operations in Fractions	Expressions and Equations	Functions	Functions
Measurement and Data	Measurement and Data	Geometry	Geometry	Modeling
Geometry	Geometry	Statistics and Probability	Statistics and Probability	Geometry
				Statistics and Probability

The charting of the domains provided the teams with powerful insights into the math CCSS. The charts were a visual verification of the progression of the domains. The color/shaded coding of the domains provided the "map" for discussions and alignment. The process of charting also created an awareness of the new vocabulary teachers needed to understand if rich, engaging lessons were to be developed.

FIGURE 10.4	Common Core State Standards Aligned Across Grade Levels			
K–2	**3–5**	**6–7**	**8**	**High School**
Counting and Cardinality (K only)				
Number and Operations in Base Ten	Number and Operations in Base Ten	The Number System	The Number System	Number and Quantity
	Number and Operations in Fractions	Ratio and Proportion		
Operations and Algebraic Thinking	Operations and Algebraic Thinking	Expressions and Equations	Expressions and Equations	Algebra
			Functions	Functions
Measurement and Data	Measurement and Data	Statistics and Probability	Statistics and Probability	Statistics and Probability
Geometry	Geometry	Geometry	Geometry	Geometry
				Modeling

Source: Adapted from initial work of Sharron Selman, math consultant.

The process for prioritizing K–8 mathematics was relatively smooth. Individuals on the K–8 teams first discussed and identified Priority Standards for their grade levels (K, 1, 2, etc.) using the principles described earlier. Next the domain was aligned by grade span (K–2, 3–5, 6–8). Teams then vertically aligned grades K–5 and 6–8. Last, K–8 met and vertically aligned the standards.

As soon as we had K–8 alignments within a domain, the 9–12 team was brought into the discussion. Each grade level described their Priority Standards to the high school team, explaining how the Priority Standards aligned, K–8. The question asked of the high school team was, "If we sent students to you who understood these *concepts* and had these *skills*, would they be prepared for success at the high school level?" If the answer was "yes," we considered the domain aligned and proceeded to the next domain. If the answer was "no," we then discussed and answered concerns to correct the issue. This process was used for each domain.

The prioritization process began with Geometry since that domain was present across all grade levels. The sequence of domains that we prioritized was as follows: Geometry, Numbers, Algebraic Thinking/Algebra, Measurement and Data, and the conceptual category of Modeling (high school only).

The high school team described the use of modeling in each domain after the other domains had been prioritized and vertically aligned. Modeling, more frequently a part of grades K–8 where mathematics instruction often utilizes real-world applications, will now need to be formally applied at all levels, K–12. The high school teams explained this meant instructional changes to include more concrete examples of mathematics in real life. This discussion revealed a pivotal point for everyone: this is new for all of us and we are all in this together.

The teams discussed the eight Standards for Mathematical Practice and decided they needed to leave them as is. Teams stated these practices should be a *point of emphasis at all times in every grade level.*

The high school team began its work using the Geometry course pathway, and the process went well. However, once discussion began about the Algebra I course pathway, the process began to "fall apart" for several reasons. Discussions about traditional Algebra I domains dominated the conversation. Issues surrounding pedagogy for instructional design as well as the appropriateness of algebra being taught at eighth grade also contributed to stalling the team's progress. Another hurdle was discussion about the revised Oregon Math Content Standards that had only recently been adopted by the state board of education as well as the state-approved instructional resources recently purchased by many districts—all done *prior to* our state's adoption of the Common Core.

The high school facilitator pointed out to the team that at this point the discussion of "how to teach" was not as important as "what is to be learned." The team had to bring the focus back to the "what" in order to proceed with the prioritization process. It was decided to focus on the domains and leave the course pathways for subsequent district or regional discussions. Focusing only on the "what is to be learned" determined by the priority criteria and principles allowed the high school team to move forward.

Prioritizing the English Language Arts CCSS

In the grade-level groups, the ELA team reviewed the format of the Common Core State Standards document, paying particular attention to the National Assessment of Educational Progress (NAEP) charts that displayed the distribution of literary and informational passages as well as the distribution of communicative purposes (Figures 10.5 and 10.6). The discussion concerning the 2009 reading framework of the NAEP brought to light that it required an increasing proportion of informational text on its assessments as students advance through the grades. The group noted that this had influenced the development of the Common Core State Standards.

FIGURE 10.5	Distribution of Literary and Informational Passages by Grade in the 2009 NAEP Reading Framework	
Grade	**Literary**	**Informational**
4	50%	50%
8	45%	55%
12	30%	70%

FIGURE 10.6	**Distribution of Communicative Purposes by Grade in the 2011 NAEP Writing Framework**

Grade	To Persuade	To Explain	To Convey Experience
4	30%	35%	35%
8	35%	35%	30%
12	40%	40%	20%

Source: National Assessment Governing Board. (2007). *Writing Framework for the 2011 National Assessment of Educational Progress* (prepublication edition). Iowa City, IA: ACT, Inc.

As facilitators of the ELA prioritization process, we also shared the breakdown of the Reading, Writing, Speaking and Listening, and Language strands to familiarize participants with the organizational structure and quantity of the Common Core standards.

Beginning with the Informational Text strand, we asked teachers to independently read and highlight their priority choices and then record them on chart-sized posters. The next step was to have groups share conversations around their collective choices and collaboratively determine the priorities for their grade level or grade span. We asked participants to pay close attention to sequencing of both skills and concepts grade-to-grade, and to identify potential gaps.

Rich conversations ensued between and among teachers regarding the content, complexity, and placement of the standards. Several issues arose and participants respectfully discussed those issues and concerns.

When the grade-level teams came together as a large K–12 group to complete the vertical alignment step of the process, there was healthy, but at times heated, conversation about where certain standards should be prioritized. One disagreement focused on which grade level should prioritize the skill of keyboarding. Teachers expressed concerns about computer availability and about the increasing demands on instructional time. After much discussion, it was agreed that keyboarding would be prioritized at the fourth-grade level, and individual districts would determine *how* keyboarding would be embedded into instruction as well as how assessment of that skill would take place.

Following the review of the CCSS Informational Text strand, grade-span groups repeated the process of individual selection, small-group discussion, and whole-group discussion and consensus of the Priority Standards identified for the Literature, Writing, Speaking and Listening, and Language strands.

The ELA process brought to light a new awareness of the breadth and depth of the Common Core State Standards. Participants took note of the Language strand of the CCSS and discussed its implications for instruction. Oregon Academic Content Standards in the areas of conventions, grammar, and vocabulary acquisition were found in the Writing and Speaking Common Core standards, but the teachers saw how much more rigorous and complex these standards were. Teachers also expressed concern over their "charge" to raise student proficiency through the grades in the area of Standard English conventions of language.

In another discussion, the entire ELA group agreed we would designate Reading Standard 10, which appears in both Informational Text and Literature, an "overarching standard" and ongoing focus at every grade. There was consensus that students need to be proficient readers at or above their grade level each year. In the midst of this process, the possibility of prioritizing some of the Foundational Skills in grades K–5 was raised. In the end it was determined that, as these are truly *foundational*, they should be taught and assessed at all grade levels, not just in grades K–5, since the grade-level rigor and complexity increases from grade to grade.

Following our two-day work session with Larry, drafts of the completed prioritized ELA Common Core State Standards were reviewed by a subset of the larger group. This group checked for alignment, gaps, and repetition. The review group asked: (1) Did the identified Priority Standards flow with clear learning progressions from grade to grade? (2) Were there similar standards at multiple grade levels that could be reclassified from Priority Standards to supporting standards? (3) Were there any gaps where we needed to strengthen instruction for skills and concepts at certain grade levels?

Completing the Process

At the end of the two days, the ELA and math teams discussed how to utilize the regional prioritized Common Core State Standards. The teams decided that these would be distributed as a "stand alone" document, a resource for the 20 districts within the region. Participating school districts were to receive copies of the final draft of the collaboratively developed Priority Common Core State Standards and follow their own process for reviewing, revising, and implementing the new Priority Standards.

To date the districts in our region have proceeded in several ways: some have used the prioritization process first and then referenced our Priority Standards documents for discussion or refinement and adoption; others have used the documents to have discussions about the CCSS, making modifications to the selections without going through the entire prioritization process; and some have used the documents for discussion and have adopted the regional Priority Standards "as is."

To assist in the process of implementing the CCSS, many of the districts have used the Navigation Tool to facilitate the discussion and analysis process with teachers.

During the school year after the process was completed (2011/12), curriculum representatives from each of our 20 school districts shared progress and implementation issues, and celebrated successes, at our regional Curriculum and Instruction meetings.

The regional prioritized math and ELA CCSS are posted on the NWRESD Web site; they can be viewed at http://et.nwresd.org. On the opening page of the site, click on "Common Core State Standards" at the left of the page; you will find the prioritized standards toward the bottom of the next page. These documents have been used not only by districts within our region, but also by other Oregon ESDs and districts as they implement the CCSS. NWRESD has received positive feedback from other educators around our state about the use of both the Navigation Tool and the Priority Standards as tools to assist in understanding and implementing the CCSS.

Next Steps

The Smarter Balanced Assessment Consortium produced their assessment "blueprint" in the past year. Our next step is to analyze the regional Priority Standards in relation to the requirements of SBAC to complete the Priority Standards process, making revisions as needed. We are planning to have small groups do this initial work and use an "accordion out" process to disseminate the information.

Participants' Comments

In debriefing participants at the end of the two days, some important ideas emerged. A few sample comments provide the flavor of the majority of the feedback. One participant stated, "I don't feel like I am alone trying to implement this anymore; I now have an understanding and the support of others that I can call on when I don't." One team commented that they now felt they could assist their districts in a "quality implementation of the CCSS." A general comment that was voiced by everyone was that "this process made what initially seemed to be an insurmountable task *possible!*"

Suggestions for Others

We have two important suggestions for those planning to prioritize the CCSS:

- Seek the assistance of consultants (professional development associates) from The Leadership and Learning Center to facilitate the process. An experienced facilitator will not make the work of prioritizing the standards easier, but will ensure that it happens effectively.

- When you get into difficult discussions or you seem to be stuck, trust the process and press ahead. When you think that the process is not working, don't panic. Keep encouraging and empowering the participants to trust their collective professional judgment—this process absolutely does work!

For more information about how the NWRESD prioritized the Common Core, please contact:

Art Anderson
Director of School Improvement and Instruction
NWRESD
5825 NE Ray Circle
Hillsboro, OR 97124
503.614.1443

Marta Turner, Pam Hallvik, Karen Durbin, Ann Kelsey
NWRESD School Improvement Specialists

Sharron Selman, Math Consultant

Art Anderson is currently a Professional Development Associate
with The Leadership and Learning Center.
He can be contacted at arthur.anderson@hmhco.com

Leadership and Learning Center Consultant:
Larry Ainsworth, larry.ainsworth@hmhco.com

CHAPTER ELEVEN

Prioritizing the CCSS: Summary of the Step-by-Step Process

Priority Standards Process at a Glance

Step 1: Make initial selections; Reach initial consensus.

Step 2: Reference SBAC Content Specifications and/or PARCC Model Content Frameworks and Publishers' Criteria; Make changes as needed.

Step 3: Chart selections for each grade.

Step 4: Vertically align Priority Standards K–12; Resolve uncertainties; Reach group consensus.

Step 5: Acquire feedback from all sites.

Step 6: Revise, publish, and distribute.

The purpose of this chapter is to provide an easy-to-reference summary of the steps any school system can follow to accomplish the identification of their Priority Common Core State Standards. Presented here are two summaries, the first for English language arts and the second for mathematics. These summarized steps, repeated from preceding chapters but without the explanatory commentary, are presented in a checklist format for easy reference by educators and leaders working through the Priority Standards process.

Following these two summaries is a third summary of the Priority Standards Steps 5 and 6 Action Plan. This summary lists the sequence of steps to follow to first *prepare* and then *implement* Steps 5 and 6 of the process.

For assistance in guiding educators and leaders through this process and beyond, you may wish to contact The Leadership and Learning Center for more information about on-site professional development.

PRIORITIZING THE ENGLISH LANGUAGE ARTS COMMON CORE STATE STANDARDS

☐ Present *rationale* for prioritizing Common Core State Standards (see key points in Chapters One and Two).

☐ Explain criteria for Priority Standards selection in English language arts:
  • Endurance, leverage, readiness for next level
  • "Fence posts"
  • Most rigorous or comprehensive

☐ Organize by grade-span groups (K–2, 3–5, 6–8, and 9–12).

☐ Select first strand to prioritize (Informational Text recommended).

☐ **Step 1:** Referring to selection criteria, make initial selections individually; reach group consensus.

☐ **Step 2:** Reference key documents for prioritization guidelines and make changes as needed:
  • SBAC Literacy Content Specifications
  • PARCC Literacy Model Content Frameworks
  • K–12 Publishers' Criteria for English Language Arts

☐ **Step 3:** Chart selections for each grade within each grade span, one chart per grade.

☐ **Step 4:** Vertically align selections K–12.
  • Grade spans post their charts in K–12 sequence.
  • Look for vertical alignment *within* grade spans.
  • Look for vertical alignment *between* grade spans (grades 2 to 3, 5 to 6, and 8 to 9).
  • Identify gaps, overlaps, and omissions.
  • Make sure learning progressions remain intact from grade to grade.
  • Identify issues to resolve with Post-It notes on charts.
  • Resolve uncertainties; revise selections as needed.
  • Repeat process with remaining strands.
  • Prepare grade-span summaries of process followed.

PRIORITIZING THE MATHEMATICS COMMON CORE STATE STANDARDS

☐ Present *rationale* for prioritizing the Common Core State Standards in Mathematics (see key points in Chapters One and Three).

☐ Explain criteria for Priority Standards selection in mathematics:

- Endurance, leverage, readiness for next level of learning
- Critical Areas of Focus for each grade
- "Fence Posts"
- Most rigorous or comprehensive

☐ Organize by grade-span groups (K–2, 3–5, 6–8, and 9–12).

☐ Select first domain to prioritize (Geometry recommended).

☐ **Step 1:** Referring to Critical Areas of Focus for each grade and domain and the prioritization criteria (endurance, leverage, readiness for next level of learning), make initial selections individually; reach group consensus.

☐ **Step 2:** Reference key documents for prioritization guidelines and make changes as needed:

- SBAC Math Content Specifications
- PARCC Model Content Math Frameworks
- Appendix A for High School Math Courses
- K–8 Publishers' Criteria for Math (particularly the section on Rigor)

☐ **Step 3:** Chart selections for each grade within each grade span, one chart per grade.

☐ **Step 4:** Vertically align selections K–12.

- Grade spans post their charts in K–12 sequence.
- Look for vertical alignment *within* grade spans.
- Look for vertical alignment *between* grade spans (grades 2 to 3, 5 to 6, and 8 to 9).
- Identify gaps, overlaps, and omissions.
- Make sure learning progressions remain intact from grade to grade.
- Identify issues to resolve with Post-It notes on charts.
- Resolve uncertainties; revise selections as needed.
- Repeat process with remaining K–8 domains and high school courses (traditional or integrated).
- Prepare grade-span summaries of process followed.

PRIORITIZING THE COMMON CORE: STEPS 5 AND 6 ACTION PLAN
(Step 5: Acquire Feedback from All;
Step 6: Revise, Publish, and Distribute)

Preparation:

☐ Create a short PowerPoint for administrators/lead teachers to present to staff.

☐ Enlist seminar participants to guide groups through the process at each school site (recommend *partnering* of facilitators for each grade span and/or entire content-area group).

☐ Prepare for school site presentations by reviewing grade-span summaries of the process followed to prioritize the math and ELA Common Core (provided by those who determined the initial selections).

☐ Plan a mini-experience of prioritizing, either with one strand of ELA and/or one domain of math, to enable colleagues to understand the process firsthand. Be sure to include the K–12 vertical alignment exercise. This will actively engage all participants and help them see how the Common Core standards connect from one grade to the next as "learning progressions."

☐ Discuss how to share the first-draft Priority Standards documents by content area (typically in grade-span or grade-level groups) to facilitate participant review.

☐ Design feedback form for groups to fill out when reviewing the first drafts (see sample in Chapter Four).

Implementation:

☐ Share information with building principals.

☐ Schedule faculty meetings to present information.

☐ Develop a plan and schedule for grade levels and departments to review Priority Standards drafts (see related items in Preparation section above).

☐ Gather revised drafts or feedback from each site.

☐ Schedule district meeting to review feedback from all sites.

☐ Prepare second drafts of Priority CCSS based on feedback.

☐ Send back to sites for final review (optional).

☐ Publish document for each content area containing *all* CCSS, with Priority Standards bolded and supporting standards in regular type.

☐ Distribute to all sites.

☐ Schedule dates for annual review/revision of Priority Standards documents, especially referencing SBAC and/or PARCC updated information.

☐ Plan related follow-up activities.

☐ Develop curriculum units of study to implement Priority Standards and supporting standards.

These are by no means all-inclusive checklists of all the activities a school system may engage in to identify and implement Priority Standards effectively in all classrooms. Their purpose is to provide you with an already-proven pathway that your own educators and leaders can follow, making whatever desired changes or modifications you decide to make along the way.

CHAPTER 12

Priority Standards— Foundation for Rigorous Curriculum Design

In *Power Standards* (2003a), I addressed two issues educators regularly raised when they completed the standards prioritization process: (1) how to sequence and schedule the Priority Standards for instruction and assessment, and (2) how to "unwrap" the Priority Standards.

Reprinted here is the text that relates to both of these issues, followed by a current, and more practical, solution to both questions set within the context of the Common Core. (Please note that I have replaced the word "power" used in the 2003 publication with the current term "priority" so as not to confuse the reader.)

Sequencing the Priority Standards

From *Power Standards* (2003a): "I ask the grade-span groups to think about their reporting periods. Whether they follow a quarterly or trimester schedule, *decide which standards should be taught in which individual reporting periods* so that there is a logical progression of when to teach which standards. Math, especially, is hierarchical. Certain concepts and skills must be taught before others if students are to truly understand them. In the same way that school systems develop a scope and sequence for the curricula, a scope and sequence can be determined for the identified Priority Standards.

"At this point, groups often choose to do a preliminary sequencing of their lists by quarter or trimester. They simply look again at their identified Priority Standards and *number them according to which ones need to be taught first, second, and so on*, to promote logical progression of student understanding."

Another Point of View Regarding Sequencing

"A middle school science educator in the Midwest brought up an excellent opposing point with regard to scheduling the Priority Standards by quarter or trimester: 'In science, I continually weave concepts and skills that I taught in an earlier unit into other units. I think it is important for students to see the connections between units of study. To slot certain standards into certain quarters defeats the idea of depth versus breadth and limits me as a science teacher as to when I can teach particular topics. The other problem is that we build our units around our sharing of instructional materials. We need to have the flexibility to teach our units in consideration of several factors.'"

Flexibility, not Restriction

"Whether a school or district chooses to sequence the Priority Standards by reporting period or not is a matter of local choice and consensus. The essential reason for prioritizing the standards is to be sure that the most important ones are identified and taught for depth of student understanding. With this shift in emphasis from 'coverage to focus,' educators find more opportunities to revisit and reemphasize those prioritized standards throughout the year and to help students make standards connections within and between content areas. The broader time frame of an entire academic school year may better afford educators the flexibility needed to accomplish this."

"Unwrapping" the Priority Standards

From *Power Standards* (2003a): "The identification of Priority Standards is often the first step school systems take in effectively implementing standards. Once this is accomplished, attention turns to aligning the Priority Standards with curriculum, instruction, and assessment. One of the most powerful practices for imparting the Priority Standards to students is called 'unwrapping' the standards.

"'Unwrapping' the standards (referring to the 2003 book by the same title) is a simple process for making standards *manageable*. I developed it in collaboration with others across the country to help educators extract from the wording of the standards the concepts and skills students need to know and be able to do. These 'unwrapped' concepts and skills are represented on a graphic organizer and then used to plan lessons, focus instruction, and drive assessment.

"Educators next identify the Big Ideas, or lasting understandings, from the 'unwrapped' concepts and skills that they want students to discover on their own and remember long after instruction ends. With these Big Ideas clearly in mind, they then formulate Essential Questions to share with students at the inception of an instructional unit. These questions guide educators in the selection of lessons and activities they will use to advance student understanding of the 'unwrapped' concepts and skills. The goal is for students to be able to answer the Essential Questions with the Big Ideas *stated in their own words* by the conclusion of an instructional unit.

"Often educators who have completed the Priority Standards identification process and later learn about 'unwrapping' the standards remark: 'We wish we had had [this] information *first*. It would have made it much easier to prioritize the standards by importance since the key concepts and skills contained within them would have been more readily apparent.'

"One process may indeed inform the other, but regardless of whichever one is experienced first, the two together make a powerful combination for improving instruction and learning."

Sequencing and "Unwrapping" the Common Core

Today educators learn how to prioritize and "unwrap" the Common Core State Standards—often in close succession, as described in two of the six district chapters within this volume. These two widespread practices work closely together to provide the focus and the specificity educators need to design effective instruction, curriculum, and assessment. The challenge in "unwrapping" and prioritizing the standards *at the same time* is that it can be an overwhelming and exceedingly time-consuming endeavor. A quicker, easier, and more manageable approach is to "unwrap" the already identified Priority Standards *within units of study* after those identified standards have been assigned to the various units at each grade level.

On their own, prioritizing and "unwrapping" can be of immense benefit to educators. However, there is a far more effective way to utilize both of these proven practices to their maximum effect—by connecting them to several *other* powerful practices used to design and then implement rigorous curricular units of study.

Priority Standards:
The Solid Foundation for Rigorous Curriculum Design

In 2010, I wrote *Rigorous Curriculum Design: How to Create Curricular Units of Study that Align Standards, Instruction, and Assessment* in response to the emerging need of school districts to revamp their existing curricula. In June of that same year, the Common Core State Standards were released, and states began rapidly adopting them. Almost overnight, the need to rewrite curricula to address the increase in rigor of the new standards became apparent. Since that time, districts across America have been implementing the RCD model as a framework for doing so. Prioritization of the Common Core is the first foundational step of that model.

In Part One of the book, "Seeing the Big Picture Connections *First*," I presented a "big picture" diagram reproduced here (Figure 12.1) that shows the deliberate connections between professional practices that educators have been using successfully for years: Priority Standards, "Unwrapping" the Standards, Common Formative Assessments, Data Teams, Effective Teaching Strategies, Authentic Performance Tasks, Scoring Guides, and others. Together, these practices create a *cohesive system* that educators are implementing over time to improve students' learning—in the classroom and in their corresponding performance on standardized tests.

Educators and leaders who are working to implement this big-picture vision in order to prepare students for success on the Common Core—as measured by their performance on the PARCC or SBAC assessments—understand that all of these interrelated practices that make up that big picture are *dependent upon a solid Priority Standards foundation.*

Rigorous Curriculum Design Model—An Overview

Since the units of study curriculum designers create will be based on the foundation of a solid set of vertically aligned Priority Standards and supporting standards, it is absolutely essential to invest the time, energy, and resources needed to establish this foundation *first*.

After the Priority Standards are selected, curriculum design teams of educators will be ready to begin the next foundational step: naming the instructional units of study. These units will "house" both the Priority Standards *and* the supporting standards. Following is a preview of the Rigorous Curriculum Design road map and its intentionally sequenced set of steps. To promote shared ownership and in-depth understanding of each of these interconnected steps, it is important that all of them be done collaboratively by teams of professional educators with as much involvement as possible by school and district leaders.

Here is an overview of Parts Two and Three of the Rigorous Curriculum Design model: "Building a Strong Curricular Foundation" and "Designing the Curricular

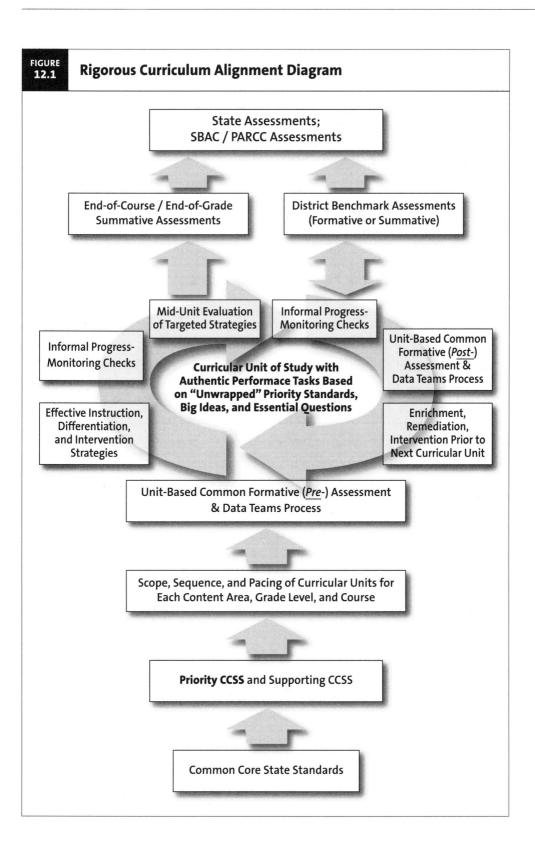

FIGURE 12.1

Rigorous Curriculum Alignment Diagram

State Assessments;
SBAC / PARCC Assessments

End-of-Course / End-of-Grade
Summative Assessments

District Benchmark Assessments
(Formative or Summative)

Mid-Unit Evaluation
of Targeted Strategies

Informal Progress-
Monitoring Checks

Informal Progress-
Monitoring Checks

Unit-Based Common
Formative (*Post*-)
Assessment &
Data Teams Process

**Curricular Unit of Study with
Authentic Performace Tasks Based
on "Unwrapped" Priority Standards,
Big Ideas, and Essential Questions**

Effective Instruction,
Differentiation,
and Intervention
Strategies

Enrichment,
Remediation,
Intervention Prior to
Next Curricular Unit

Unit-Based Common Formative (*Pre-*) Assessment
& Data Teams Process

Scope, Sequence, and Pacing of Curricular Units for
Each Content Area, Grade Level, and Course

Priority CCSS and Supporting CCSS

Common Core State Standards

Units of Study," respectively. Notice that "Unwrap" the Unit Priority Standards is the first of twelve unit design steps in Part Three. Part Four explains "How to Implement Each Unit of Study." Each step of the entire process is explained in detail with examples in its corresponding chapter of *Rigorous Curriculum Design*.

BUILD A STRONG CURRICULAR FOUNDATION (5 Steps)

Before constructing the curricular units of study, it is necessary to first build a strong foundation. Otherwise, curriculum design teams are erecting a superstructure upon an uncertain base. Following is a brief description of each of the five foundational steps:

1. **Prioritize the Standards.** Prioritize and vertically align from grade to grade and course to course the academic content standards (grade- or course-specific CCSS and/or state standards) for selected content areas. These represent the "assured competencies" that students are to know and be able to do by the end of each academic school year so they are prepared to enter the *next* level of learning.

2. **Name the Units of Study.** Name all of the specific units of study for each grade level and course in the selected content areas. Through these units of study, implemented during the year or course, students will learn and be assessed upon their understanding and application of the particular standards in focus.

3. **Assign Priority Standards and Supporting Standards.** Assign Priority Standards *and* supporting standards to each unit of study, taking into account "learning progressions"—those building blocks of concepts and skills that students need to learn before they can learn other ones.

4. **Prepare a Pacing Calendar.** Referring to the school district master calendar, create a curriculum pacing calendar for implementing the units of study to ensure that all Priority Standards will be taught, assessed, retaught, and reassessed throughout the school year. Factor in a "buffer" week (two or more days, up to five) *between* units for the purpose of reteaching and reassessing close-to-proficient students, intervening and reassessing far-from-proficient students, and enriching proficient and above students. Adjust the length and/or duration of each unit of study so that all of the units can be implemented before the end of the school year.

5. **Construct the Unit Planning Organizer.** Brainstorm a list of elements to include on a unit planning organizer that will be used to create each unit of study. Draft

a sample template that includes all of these elements. Revise the template as needed while designing the curricular units.

DESIGN THE CURRICULAR UNITS, FROM START TO FINISH (12 Steps)

With the standards foundation in place, design each curricular unit of study, from start to finish. Here is a synopsis of each of the 12 sequential steps for doing so. Be sure all of these elements (except the weekly and daily planners) appear on the agreed-upon unit planning organizer.

1. **"Unwrap" the Unit Priority Standards.** "Unwrap" the assigned Priority Standards within *each individual unit of study* to determine the specific, teachable concepts and skills (what students need to know and be able to do) in those standards.

2. **Create a Graphic Organizer.** Create a graphic organizer (outline, bulleted list, concept map, or chart) as a visual display of the "unwrapped" concepts and skills, organized into two parts: one that lists related concepts under headings and the other that lists each skill, related concept, and *approximate* levels of Bloom's Taxonomy and Webb's Depth of Knowledge. Matching each skill and related concept with the thinking skill levels reveals the skill's degree of *rigor.*

3. **Decide the Big Ideas and Essential Questions.** Decide the topical Big Ideas (key understandings, student "aha's") derived from the "unwrapped" concepts and skills for that unit of study. Write Essential Questions that will engage students to discover for themselves the related Big Ideas and state them in their own words by the end of the unit.

4. **Create the End-of-Unit Assessment.** Create the end-of-unit assessment (either individual classroom or common formative post-assessment) *directly aligned* to the "unwrapped" Priority Standards and their levels of rigor. Align the concepts, skills, and format of the end-of-unit assessment with district or school benchmark assessments (K–8) or midterms and finals/end-of-course exams (9–12).

5. **Create the Unit Pre-Assessment.** Create the pre-assessment aligned or "mirrored" to the post-assessment. "Aligned" means the questions are directly matched to those on the post-assessment but may be fewer in number. "Mirrored" means the pre-assessment will be the exact replica of the number and types of questions that will appear on the post-assessment.

6. **Identify Additional Vocabulary Terms, Interdisciplinary Connections, and 21st-Century Learning Skills.** In addition to the vocabulary of the "unwrapped" Priority Standards concepts, identify other specific academic or technical vocabulary from the supporting standards and text materials that students will need to learn during the unit. Identify any interdisciplinary connections and 21st-century learning skills to emphasize when planning engaging learning experiences and related instruction.

7. **Plan Engaging Learning Experiences.** Design meaningful learning activities directly based upon the "unwrapped" concepts and skills, additional vocabulary terms, interdisciplinary connections, and 21st-century learning skills. Plan engaging learning experiences—authentic performance tasks with real-world applications—that challenge students to utilize deep thought, investigation, and communication. Create accompanying scoring guides (rubrics) as the means for obtaining objective evidence of student learning relative to the standards in focus. Confirm that the planned learning experiences will give students the conceptual and procedural understanding of the "unwrapped" concepts, skills, and levels of rigor they will need to be successful on the end-of-unit post-assessment. These carefully planned learning tasks should be designed to "deliver" students to the Big Ideas of the unit.

8. **Gather Resource Materials.** Gather print materials and seek out technology resources that support the planned learning experiences for the unit. Select the most appropriate instructional resources and materials available that will assist students in learning and applying the "unwrapped" concepts and skills and discovering the Big Ideas.

9. **Select High-Impact Instructional Strategies.** Select high-impact instructional strategies (research-based, differentiation, enrichment, intervention, special education, English Language Learner, others) that teachers can use during instruction and related learning activities with the whole class, with small groups, and with individual students who have specific learning needs.

10. **Detail the Unit Planning Organizer.** Determine what additional details are needed to supplement the generally worded information on the unit planning organizer. For example, an instructional pacing and sequence of the "unwrapped" concepts and skills based on "learning progressions" (the sequence of concepts and skills students need to know and be able to do as prerequisites

for learning the next set of concepts and skills); a listing of specific instructional strategies for specific students based on their learning needs (advanced students, at-risk students, special education students, English Language Learners) along with suggestions for how to use them.

11. **Create Informal Progress-Monitoring Checks.** Find, design, or suggest quick, informal checks for student understanding (exit slips, short-answer questions, thumbs up/down, etc.)—*aligned to the end-of-unit assessment and administered in conjunction with "learning progressions"*—for educators to use during the unit of study in order to gauge student understanding and adjust instruction accordingly.

12. **Write the Weekly Plan; Design the Daily Lessons*.** Write the weekly lesson plan to implement the unit of study in weekly "installments," using it to guide and focus instruction of the targeted "unwrapped" concepts and skills and engage students in the planned learning experiences and assessments. Design the daily lessons to align with the related weekly plan.

HOW TO IMPLEMENT EACH UNIT OF STUDY (14 Steps)

When the unit planning organizers are completed and ready to use, implement each of the units according to the scheduled pacing calendars. Here is a brief description of the 14 steps for doing so:

1. **Introduce the Unit of Study to Students.** Present the unit's Essential Questions to students and explain that they will be able to respond to these questions in their own words by the end of the unit. Preview for students the "unwrapped" concepts and other academic vocabulary terms they will be learning and applying.

2. **Administer the Unit Pre-Assessment.** Set the stage by first explaining to students the purpose of a pre-assessment (not for a grade, but to find out what they already know and don't know about the upcoming unit of study so that the teacher can plan instruction accordingly). Then administer the common formative pre-assessment (or individual classroom or program pre-assessment, if not part of a collaborative team).

---

*To be completed by classroom teachers, not the curriculum design teams.

3. **Score and Analyze Student Data.** Score and analyze student pre-assessments individually or with colleagues in grade-level or course-specific instructional Data Teams to diagnose student learning needs.

4. **Decide How to Differentiate Instruction.** Referring to the unit details provided with the unit planning organizer, decide how to differentiate instruction for specific students based on pre-assessment evidence—including the enrichment of any students who are already proficient prior to unit instruction.

5. **Begin Teaching the Unit.** Begin teaching the planned unit of study, flexibly grouping students according to their learning needs and using identified instructional strategies.

6. **Administer Progress-Monitoring Checks.** Administer frequent, informal progress-monitoring checks aligned to the end-of-unit assessment—that coincide with the building-block progression of "unwrapped" concepts and skills—in order to make accurate inferences regarding students' understanding. These informal checks will assist individual educators and instructional Data Teams in monitoring the effectiveness of their targeted teaching strategies for the unit.

7. **Differentiate Instruction Based on Progress-Monitoring Checks.** Modify and adjust instruction for individual students, small groups, and/or the entire class based on the results of the informal checks for understanding.

8. **Schedule Mid-Unit Evaluation of Instructional Strategies.** Schedule a mid-unit evaluation of the targeted teaching and differentiation strategies to determine their effectiveness. During this meeting, participating teachers will share effective use of the targeted strategies and may decide to change any strategies that are not accomplishing their intended purpose. Individual educators who are not part of an instructional Data Team will reflect on the effectiveness of their own selected strategies and make any needed changes.

9. **Continue Teaching the Unit.** During the remaining weeks of the unit, continue teaching the "unwrapped" concepts and skills in the predetermined "learning progressions" sequence for specific learning activities and engaging learning experiences (authentic performance tasks). Continue using the targeted instructional strategies with all students, different groups of students, and individual students as planned.

10. **Continue Modifying and Adjusting Instruction.** Continue modifying and adjusting instruction as needed for individual students, small groups, and/or the entire class based on evidence derived from ongoing progress-monitoring checks.

11. **Administer End-of-Unit Assessment.** Administer the common formative post-assessment (or individual end-of-unit assessment if not part of a collaborative team).

12. **Score and Analyze Student Data.** Score and analyze student data individually or with colleagues in grade-level or course-specific instructional Data Teams. Celebrate successes! Plan how to address students' identified learning needs during the "buffer" days/week.

13. **Enrich, Remediate, and Intervene.** During the "buffer" days/week scheduled between the unit of study just completed and the next one scheduled, reteach *differently* those students who are still not proficient; use Tier 2 and 3 intervention strategies and other appropriate strategies for at-risk students. Reassess all non-proficient students. Enrich those students who are proficient and advanced.

14. **Reflect and Begin Again.** When the unit is officially completed, reflect individually and/or with colleagues about what worked well and what, if anything, should be changed the next time the unit is implemented. Take a deep breath, redirect your focus, and then repeat the process with the next unit of study.

Conclusion

Driven by the rigorous demands of the Common Core, each school and school district must now make many changes in curriculum, instructional practices, assessment, data analysis, and the reporting of student progress. But these changes will, over time, continue to inspire educators toward the goal of all educational restructuring—that of achieving increased student success in school, improved student performance on all assessment measures, and a more effective preparation of students for college, career, and adult life.

The Common Core State Standards are, by themselves, insufficient. Its authors asserted this in the following statement: "To be effective in improving education and getting all students ready for college, workforce training, and life, the Common Core State Standards must be partnered with a content-rich curriculum and robust assess-

ments, both aligned to the Standards" (CCSS Webinar, 2010: Last slide of www
.corestandards.org/assets/Common_Core_Standards_June_2010_Webinar_Final_v
_2.ppt).

Prioritizing the Common Core State Standards is only the first step in "partnering" and "aligning" those standards with curriculum and assessments. Following this
must be those *other steps* for designing and implementing rigorous curricular units
of study based on that strong standards foundation. This is the big-picture vision—
a carefully constructed "road map" with designated milestones to reach over time—
a marathon, not a sprint.

Someone once said, "All grand visions come dressed up in work clothes." This is
indeed a lot of work, and it is important to acknowledge this up front with educators who gather to *do* this work. Yet when the work of prioritizing the Common
Core and redesigning the curricula is finished, educators will have created, through
a shared-ownership process, a dynamic set of curricular "products" that everyone
can use to improve instruction and student achievement for many years to come. So
"keep on keeping on" toward the accomplishment of this grand vision!

REFERENCES

Ainsworth, L. (2003a). *Power standards: Identifying the standards that matter the most.* Englewood, CO: Advanced Learning Press.

Ainsworth, L. (2003b). *"Unwrapping" the standards: A simple process to make standards manageable.* Englewood, CO: Advanced Learning Press.

Ainsworth, L. (2010). *Rigorous curriculum design: How to create curricular units of study that align standards, instruction, and assessment.* Englewood, CO: Lead + Learn Press.

Christinson, J. (2012). How the K–8 learning progressions influence planning for instruction and assessment. In J. Christinson, et al., *Navigating the mathematics common core state standards.* Englewood, CO: Lead + Learn Press.

Common Core State Standards Initiative (CCSSI). (2010a). *Common core state standards for English language arts & literacy in history/social studies, science, and technical subjects* (PDF document). Retrieved from www.corestandards.org/assets/CCSSI_ELA%20Standards.pdf

Common Core State Standards Initiative (CCSSI). (2010b). *Common core state standards for English language arts & literacy in history/social studies, science, and technical subjects: Appendix A* (PDF document). Retrieved from www.corestandards.org/assets/ Appendix_A.pdf

Common Core State Standards Initiative (CCSSI). (2010c). *Common core state standards for English language arts & literacy in history/social studies, science, and technical subjects: Appendix B* (PDF document). Retrieved from www.corestandards.org/assets/ Appendix_B.pdf

Common Core State Standards Initiative (CCSSI). (2010d). *Common core state standards for mathematics* (PDF document). Retrieved from www.corestandards.org/assets/CCSSI _Math%20Standards.pdf

Common Core State Standards Initiative (CCSSI). (2010e). *Common core state standards for mathematics: Appendix A* (PDF document). Retrieved from www.corestandards.org/assets/ CCSSI_Mathematics_Appendix_A.pdf

DuFour, R., DuFour, R., Eaker, R., & Many, T. (2010). *Learning by doing: A handbook for professional learning communities at work.* (2nd ed.). Bloomington, IN: Solution Tree.

Fisher, D., & Frey, N. (2008). *Better learning through structured teaching: A framework for the gradual release of responsibility.* Alexandria, VA: ASCD.

Hess, K. K. (2011). *Learning progressions frameworks designed for use with the common core state standards in English language arts & literacy K–12* (PDF document). Retrieved from http://www.naacpartners.org/publications/ELA_LPF_12.2011_final.pdf

Jacobs, H. H. (1997). *Mapping the big picture: Integrating curriculum and assessment K–12.* Alexandria, VA: ASCD.

Klein, A. (2008, September 24). Groups seek to keep a spotlight on issues of testing, standards. *Education Week,* p. 24.

Marzano, R. J. (2003). *What works in schools: Translating research into action.* Alexandria, VA: ASCD.

Popham, W. J. (2003). *Test better, teach better: The instructional role of assessment.* Alexandria, VA: ASCD.

Popham, W. J. (2004, November). Curriculum matters. *American School Board Journal,* p. 31.

Reeves, D. B. (1997). *Making standards work: How to implement standards-based assessments in the classroom, school, and district.* Englewood, CO: Advanced Learning Press.

Reeves, D. B. (2001). *101 questions & answers about standards, assessment, and accountability.* Englewood, CO: Advanced Learning Press.

Reeves, D. B. (2004). *Accountability in action: A blueprint for learning organizations.* Englewood, CO: Advanced Learning Press.

Schmoker, M. (2011). *Focus: Elevating the essentials to radically improve student learning.* Alexandria, VA: ASCD.

Sherer, M. (2001). How and why standards can improve student achievement: A conversation with Robert J. Marzano. *Educational Leadership, 59*(1), 14–18.

Wiggs, M. D. (2011). Gaining a deeper understanding of the common core state standards: The big picture. In D. B. Reeves, et al., *Navigating implementation of the common core state standards.* Englewood, CO: Lead + Learn Press.

INDEX